I0820097

5-Ingredient Mediterranean Cookbook

5-Ingredient Mediterranean Cookbook

Amazingly Healthy Quick-Fix Meals

Editors of the Harvard Common Press

HARVARD
COMMON
PRESS

Quarto.com

First Published in 2026 by The Harvard Common Press, an imprint of The Quarto Group,
100 Cummings Center, Suite 265-D, Beverly, MA 01915, USA.
T (978) 282-9590 F (978) 283-2742

EEA Representation, WTS Tax d.o.o.,
Žanova ulica 3, 4000 Kranj, Slovenia.
www.wts-tax.si

The Harvard Common Press titles are also available at discount for retail, wholesale, promotional, and bulk purchase. For details, contact the Special Sales Manager by email at specialsales@quarto.com or by mail at The Quarto Group, Attn: Special Sales Manager, 100 Cummings Center, Suite 265-D, Beverly, MA 01915, USA.

30 29 28 27 26 2 3 4 5

ISBN: 978-1-57715-574-4

Digital edition published in 2026
eISBN: 978-1-57715-575-1

The content in this book was previously published in *Clean Eating Kitchen: The Low-Carb Mediterranean Cookbook* (Fair Winds Press 2021) by Michelle Dudash; *Mediterranean Small Plates* (Harvard Common Press 2022) by Clifford A. Wright; and *The Ultimate Mediterranean Diet Cookbook* (Fair Winds Press 2015) by Amy Riolo.

Library of Congress Cataloging-in-Publication Data is available

Design and Page Layout: Laura Klynstra

Printed in Huizhou City, Guangdong, China TT022026

A Note about "Five Ingredients"

"Five-ingredient recipes" have long been a favorite among home cooks. In creating recipes that fit this description, cookbook publishers, food magazines, and other food media traditionally exclude the following when counting the number of ingredients: salt, pepper, cooking oils (including butter), and water. We follow this well-established practice in this book, too. If you see a recipe that appears to have more than five ingredients, the "extras" will be from this list of excluded ingredients.

Contents

CHAPTER 4

Vegetable Sides ✲ 85

CHAPTER 5

Protein-Powered Entrees ✲ 115

CHAPTER 6

Sweets and Desserts ✱ 157

INTRODUCTION

A Concise Guide to the Mediterranean Diet

The Mediterranean diet is known as the healthiest in the world because it is not truly a diet, but rather a lifestyle that prescribes a lot of what we should eat, and a little of what we shouldn't, along with shared physical and social activities. Oldways, a nonprofit food and nutrition education organization, refers to the Mediterranean diet as "the gold standard eating pattern that promotes lifelong good health."

The Mediterranean diet is a modern eating plan based on the traditional diet and lifestyle of the countries bordering the Mediterranean Sea. Best of all, while many of the recipes, ingredients, and traditions celebrated in the Mediterranean diet have been around for centuries, they are easily adaptable into today's busy lifestyle and suitable for modern palates. There are no fads, special "diet" foods, or modern technology needed to achieve successful results. There are no formulas, exchanges, or point systems to master. Best of all, you don't need a nutrition label to determine what fits into the lifestyle. Centered on healthful, whole foods eaten in moderation, sticking to the Mediterranean diet becomes second nature.

The Science Behind the Diet

Intrigued by the number of elderly people living with lower rates of illness and disease in the region, scientists and doctors around the world have been researching the Mediterranean diet for more than half a century. Today, large well-designed studies and clinical trials are demonstrating its effects. Following the diet has thus far been linked to:

- preventing heart attacks and strokes
- improved mental capacity
- preventing and reversing diabetes
- reversing the symptoms and reducing the incidence of Parkinson's and Alzheimer's
- longevity
- reduced inflammation
- reduced risk of death from heart disease and cancer
- preventing cancer and inhibiting tumor growth

One impressive study of 7,447 people reported in 2013 in *The New England Journal of Medicine* found that high-risk heart disease subjects could prevent 30 percent of heart attacks, strokes, and deaths from heart disease by switching to a Mediterranean diet. The results were so dramatic that the study was concluded early because the researchers felt that continuing to test control groups following other diets would be unethical when they had already determined the efficacy of the diet.

Another study published in the *Annals of Internal Medicine* tracked the diets and lifestyles of more than 10,000 women in their fifties for fifteen years. The results showed that 40 percent of those who followed the Mediterranean diet were more likely to live past the age of seventy without chronic diseases, memory loss, or physical problems. They also suffered fewer strokes and were less likely to die than the control group who simply followed a low-fat diet.

It is worth noting that low-fat and Mediterranean diets have different philosophies. Low-fat diets focus on what people should not eat (namely, fat), whereas the notion of deprivation does not fit with the tenets of the Mediterranean diet. So, while following a generally low-fat diet may cut risks associated with higher fat intakes, you will not reap the same rewards that the Mediterranean diet offers.

Many doctors are recommending the Mediterranean diet for combating chronic inflammation, which is an underlying cause or factor in many illnesses, from allergies and arthritis to autoimmune diseases and even cancer. To prove that the Mediterranean diet can reduce inflammation and impact diabetes, Spanish researchers studied 3,541 Spaniards between the ages of fifty-five and eighty who had three or more risk factors for diabetes. After four years, 87 percent of the high-risk subjects following a Mediterranean diet were able to prevent the onset of diabetes.

The combination of a lifetime of enjoyable meals that taste great and just happen to be good for you is almost too good to be true! One of the most attractive attributes of the diet is that, in essence, it doesn't ask us to give up anything or deprive ourselves: It's a simple strategy that requires exercise, consuming the majority of calories from foods that are good for you, and reserving those that aren't for special occasions.

It's a Lifestyle

It might come as a surprise to many that the base of the Mediterranean Diet Pyramid is not a food group at all, but rather behaviors such as physical activity and social interaction. At its core, the Mediterranean diet is not a diet in the conventional sense of the word. It is a lifestyle that should be enjoyed with both pleasure and health in mind. When people sit down at a table in Egypt, the phrase *bilhanna wi shefa* or "with pleasure and health" is uttered much in the same way that bon appétit is in many places. Food should be about equal parts health and enjoyment.

THE MEDITERRANEAN, IN A NUTSHELL

The Mediterranean region is made up of the countries and islands that touch the Mediterranean Sea. These nations include Spain, France, Italy, Croatia, Albania, and Greece on its northern edge, and Turkey, Syria, Lebanon, and Israel to the east; Egypt, Libya, Tunisia, Algeria, and Morocco to the south; and the region is also sprinkled with many islands large and small, such as Corsica (French), Sardinia (Italian), Sicily (Italian), Majorca (Spanish), Malta, Crete, Cyprus, and all the Greek Islands. The Mediterranean has hot and dry summers and cool, humid winters. Much of the landscape is hilly and dry, which are ideal conditions for growing the olives, grapes, dates, apricots, pistachios, and other fruits and nuts that feature prominently in Mediterranean cuisine. Being a large inland sea surrounded by three continents, the Mediterranean can boast seafood in a variety of species and styles.

PHYSICAL ACTIVITY

The Mediterranean's philosophy of approaching life with an equal measure of pleasure and health leads to a more balanced and happy existence. To the majority of people living in modern urban areas, physical activity means heading off to a gym to work off calories on machines after an entire day's worth of sitting at their desks, in their cars, or on their couches.

In the Mediterranean region, however, it's another story. Daily life is set up to naturally require more activity and calorie expenditure. Urban and commercial areas are built in historic centers that preceded the invention of cars. Driving and parking in them is difficult, which necessitates a greater deal of walking. Electrical capacity is also often lower in many areas, making it difficult to operate many appliances simultaneously. Outside of hotels, few people have clothes dryers, even in urban areas. Simple tasks such as hanging clothes out to dry and ironing them, shopping, and cooking require greater effort and expenditure of calories.

In order to enjoy optimal health and reap the rewards of the Mediterranean diet, followers need to integrate pleasurable forms of activity into their daily lives.

CAMARADERIE

Every country and culture around the Mediterranean has its own way of encouraging people to eat together, and family life is valued greatly. Throughout the region's history, eating alone was frowned upon. Only unworthy bachelors or scorned people who didn't have family would eat by themselves. While attitudes have changed in modern times, most people in the Mediterranean find it unpleasant to eat alone. Fortunately, in many places, work and school schedules revolve around mealtimes. When they do not, families change their schedules in order to be able to eat together at least for one meal per day.

Residents on the Mediterranean island of Sardinia are ten times more likely to live past 100 than people in the United States. Researchers who studied this remarkable longevity found that daily communal (family style) eating was commonplace and attributed it to the overall well-being of residents. The researchers concluded that there is something extremely satisfying and comforting about knowing that, no matter how difficult life gets, at lunchtime you will be surrounded by loved ones. This adds a deep sense of psychological security, which, in turn, has a positive effect on health and happiness.

GROUND RULES FOR REWARDING FAMILY MEALS

1. No television or electronics.
2. No off-limits or unpleasant topics.
3. Dress for the meal.
4. Set as attractive a table as possible.
5. Discuss pleasant topics and good news.

Throughout the region, food is viewed as a way to express love, thanks, appreciation, and respect. It may be used as a gift, as a way to settle a debt, or as traditional medicine. In southern European countries such as Spain, Italy, Greece, and France, great pride is taken in giving a guest or a loved one a handmade food item; if it was grown on the giver's own land, it is even more special. What comes from the hands is an extension of self—and is healthier than what can be bought at the store.

In our busy day-to-day existence, much of what is described here might sound like a Utopian fantasy. While most Americans will find re-creating this type of lifestyle unrealistic, there are simple ways to implement it:

- Vow to live each day with both pleasure and health in mind.
- Find easy, enjoyable ways to get more exercise, such as gardening or walking with a friend.
- Begin incorporating new and varied plant-based foods into your diet.
- Identify simple, make-ahead dishes and snacks to work into your schedule.
- If it is not already a custom, make plans to eat, exercise, and socialize with friends, family, and co-workers as often as possible.
- Treat food, family, and friends as if they are the most important part of your life.

CHAPTER 1

Breads

Whole-Wheat Pita Bread

Whole-wheat pita bread dates back to the twentieth century BCE in ancient Egypt. Under Roman rule, wheat flour from Egypt and North Africa was exported throughout the Roman Empire, and similar recipes spread throughout the Mediterranean. The Roman philosopher Apicius even mentioned the "bread from Alexandria" in his cookbook *De Re Coquinaria.*

TOTAL PREP AND COOK TIME: 3 hours	**YIELD:** 6 Pitas

1⅛ cups (265 ml) warm water

1 tablespoon (12 g) active dry yeast

½ tablespoon (9 g) unrefined sea salt or salt

2 cups (250 g) whole-wheat flour (see Gluten-Free Alternative)

1½ cups (188 g) unbleached, all-purpose flour (see Gluten-Free Alternative)

1 tablespoon (15 ml) extra-virgin olive oil

1. Pour the water into a large bowl. Add the yeast and stir until dissolved. Add the salt, and gradually incorporate the flours to form a dough.
2. Turn the dough out onto a lightly floured work surface and knead for 10 minutes, until smooth and elastic. Or place in the bowl of an electric mixer fitted with a hook attachment and knead on medium speed for 2 minutes.
3. Pour the oil into a bowl and place dough inside the bowl, turning to coat. Cover with oiled plastic and a kitchen towel and let rise until doubled in bulk (1½ to 2 hours).
4. When the dough has risen, punch down gently. Divide the dough into six equal portions and shape into balls. Place on a lightly floured surface and cover with a dry kitchen towel. Let rest for 15 minutes.
5. Preheat the oven to 475°F (240°C). Place a baking stone or sheet in lowest section of oven. Roll out each dough circle to form a 6-inch (15 cm) circle. Place three circles on the preheated baking sheet and bake for about 12 minutes (until they are puffed up and begin to turn color). Refrain from opening the oven during the first 4 minutes of cooking. Remove with a metal spatula or pizza peel and place in a bread basket or on a serving platter. Repeat with the remaining dough circles until all are baked.

GLUTEN-FREE ALTERNATIVE:
Replace the flours in this recipe with a combination of 1½ cups (237 g) brown rice flour, 1 cup (125 g) tapioca flour, 1 cup (136 g) sorghum flour, and 2 teaspoons xanthan gum.

Mediterranean Tradition

Fresh breads go stale quickly because they lack the preservatives that give commercial breads a longer shelf life. For that reason, savvy cooks in the region have been utilizing day-old breads in countless ways for millennia. Try cutting this day-old bread into cubes, drizzling it with olive oil, and sprinkling with za'atar spice or Pecorino Romano cheese. Place on a baking sheet and toast in a 400°F (200°C) oven until golden. The croutons are a perfect addition to salads, soups, stews, and casseroles.

PER SERVING: 270 CALORIES | 52 G CARBOHYDRATE (5 G FIBER | 0 G ADDED SUGARS | 47 G NET CARBS) | 9 G PROTEIN | 3.5 G FAT | 590 MG SODIUM

Mediterranean-Style Cornbread

Even though corn is native to the Americas, its popularity in the Mediterranean region is so widespread that you would think it originated there. This Italian-inspired version is an updated interpretation of traditional recipes from the northern Italian regions of Veneto, Lombardia, and Friuli. Introduced by the Ottomans in the 900s, corn flour was called *granoturco*, or "Turkish grains" in Italian, and became extremely popular with the Jewish community in Venice. Soon thereafter, it became a poor man's staple throughout Italy.

TOTAL PREP AND COOK TIME: 1 hour | **YIELD:** 12 servings

2 teaspoons extra-virgin olive oil, divided

2½ cups (305 g) stone-ground 100% whole-grain, medium-grind cornmeal

½ tablespoon (9 g) unrefined sea salt or salt

2 teaspoons baking powder

1 teaspoon sugar

2 cups (475 ml) boiling water

¼ cup (14 g) chopped sun-dried tomatoes

4 ounces (115 g) fresh mozzarella cheese, shredded by hand into large pieces

1. Preheat the oven to 350°F (180°C).
2. Grease an 8-inch (20 cm) round cake pan with 1 teaspoon olive oil.
3. Combine the cornmeal, salt, remaining 1 teaspoon olive oil, baking powder, and sugar in a large bowl. Add the boiling water and stir to mix until all of the water is incorporated in the mixture.
4. Stir in the sun-dried tomatoes and mozzarella. Pour the cornmeal mixture into the prepared pan. Wet your hands and press down to smooth the top.
5. Bake for 10 minutes and then cover the pan with aluminum foil and bake for 20 to 30 minutes, or until golden and firm on top. Allow to cool slightly and serve warm, or allow to cool and wrap in plastic wrap.

Mediterranean Tradition

While many Americans find the words healthful bread *to be an oxymoron, this isn't the case in the Mediterranean region. There, fresh breads made with high-quality grains are enjoyed daily and are a backbone to the diet. Simple, quick breads such as this one can be whipped up in minutes and provide a heartier alternative to store-bought varieties.*

PER SERVING: 150 CALORIES | 27 G CARBOHYDRATE (3 G FIBER | 0 G ADDED SUGARS | 23 G NET CARBS) | 4 G PROTEIN | 3.5 G FAT | 410 MG SODIUM

Whole-Wheat and Grape Focaccia

Schiacciata, the name of this delicious bread in Italian, is derived from the verb *schiacciare*, which means "flattened out," and that's exactly what happens when freshly harvested grapes are pressed into it. Traditionally made at grape harvest time in Tuscany, this recipe originated with the Etruscans and was baked in the ashes of an open hearth.

TOTAL PREP AND COOK TIME: 2½ hours **YIELD:** 8 to 10 servings

1½ cups (355 ml) warm water

½ cup (120 ml) Vin Santo (Italian dessert wine)

1 package (¼ ounce, or 7 g) active dry yeast

½ cup (118 ml) extra-virgin olive oil, divided, plus extra for greasing pan

3 cups (375 g) whole-wheat flour (see Gluten-Free Alternative)

1 cup (125 g) unbleached, all-purpose flour (see Gluten-Free Alternative)

1 teaspoon unrefined sea salt or salt

2 cups (300 g) seedless red grapes, cut in half lengthwise

1. Pour the water and Vin Santo in the bowl of a standing mixer. Sprinkle the yeast over the top, and mix using the paddle attachment until combined. Let set for 5 minutes. Pour in ¼ cup (60 ml) of olive oil. Add the whole-wheat flour and mix on low speed. Slowly add in the all-purpose flour and salt, and mix until well combined.

2. Switch to the dough hook attachment and knead the dough on medium speed for 5 minutes. Cover the bowl with oiled plastic wrap and allow to rest at room temperature until doubled in size, about 1 hour (see note).

3. Oil a 13 x 17-inch (33 x 43 cm) rimmed baking sheet. Turn the dough from the bowl onto the baking sheet. Stretch the dough out and press down until it covers the surface of the pan in an even layer.

4. Using all the fingers of your hands, press down to make dimples in the surface of the focaccia. Cover with oiled plastic wrap and allow to rest for 30 minutes, or until the dough has doubled in size again.

5. Preheat the oven to 425°F (220°C).

6. Before baking, brush the surface of the focaccia with the remaining ¼ cup (60 ml) of olive oil. Scatter the grapes, cut side down over the top and press them down slightly. Bake for 30 to 35 minutes, or until the

PER SERVING: 380 CALORIES | 53 G CARBOHYDRATE (6 G FIBER | 0 G ADDED SUGARS | 47 G NET CARBS) | 8 G PROTEIN | 15 G FAT | 300 MG SODIUM

focaccia turns a nice golden brown and is cooked through. Remove from the oven and allow to cool slightly. Cut and serve immediately. Leftover, cooled pieces can be wrapped in plastic wrap and frozen for up to 1 month.

GLUTEN-FREE ALTERNATIVE:
Substitute the flour in this recipe with 1½ cups (188 g) tapioca flour, 1⅓ cups (181 g) sorghum flour, ⅔ cup (129 g) potato starch, ½ cup (79 g) sweet rice flour, and 1 teaspoon xanthan gum.

NOTE: *If you would like to make this dough in the morning to eat in the evening, cover the bowl with plastic wrap and a clean kitchen towel and place in the refrigerator. In 12 hours, you will have the same results as if it sat at room temperature for 1 hour.*

Mediterranean Tradition

Using fresh fruit in as many ways possible is something that chefs and home cooks in the Mediterranean region take great pride in. Challenge yourself to go outside of your culinary comfort zone when garden-fresh fruits are readily available—you'll be sure to discover new favorites and increase your plant–based food intake.

Whole-Wheat Country Moroccan Bread

This easy bread, often made with barley, has a soft, moist crumb. It is a Moroccan recipe, and it's a great bread for any meal. It is best eaten the day it is made, or frozen, then defrosted and reheated the day it is served. Freeze by wrapping it in plastic wrap and then aluminum foil. Thaw at room temperature and warm in a preheated 350°F (180°C) oven before serving.

TOTAL PREP AND COOK TIME: 1¾ hours **YIELD:** 3 round loaves

2½ cups (591 ml) warm water

1 tablespoon (12 g) active dry yeast

2 teaspoons sugar

1 teaspoon kosher salt

6 to 8 cups (750 g to 1 kg) whole-wheat or barley flour, plus extra for kneading (see Gluten-Free Alternative)

4 teaspoons (20 ml) extra-virgin olive oil, divided

3 teaspoons (8 g) sesame seeds

GLUTEN-FREE ALTERNATIVE: *Replace whole-wheat flour with a combination of 3 to 5 cups (474 to 790 g) brown rice flour, 1 cup (125 g) tapioca flour, 2 cups (272 g) sorghum flour, and 2 teaspoons xanthan gum.*

1. Pour the warm water into the bowl of a standing electric mixer with a paddle attachment. Sprinkle the yeast and sugar over the water, and mix until dissolved.
2. Add the salt and gradually mix in 6 cups (750 g) of flour, adding up to 2 more cups, one cup (125 g) at a time, until dough pulls away from the side of the bowl.
3. Switch to a hook attachment and knead for 5 minutes on medium speed, or until smooth.
4. Roll the dough into a 12-inch (30 cm) log, then divide into three equal pieces. Shape each piece into a 4-inch (10 cm) dome-shaped loaf. Place loaves on a baking sheet greased with 1 teaspoon oil. Cover with a kitchen towel and place in a draft-free area to rise for 1 hour, or until doubled.
5. Preheat the oven to 350°F (180°C). Uncover the loaves and brush each with 1 teaspoon olive oil and 1 teaspoon sesame seeds. Bake for 20 to 30 minutes, or until lightly golden. Let cool slightly, and serve warm.

PER SERVING: 60 CALORIES | 13 G CARBOHYDRATE (2 G FIBER | 0 G ADDED SUGARS | 11 G NET CARBS) | 2 G PROTEIN | 1 G FAT | 40 MG SODIUM

Mediterranean Tradition

One of the earliest cultivated grains, barley is a member of the grass family and has been cultivated since the ninth millennium BCE. Its production boomed after the second millennium BCE in Mesopotamia, and it became a popular, inexpensive, and nutritious ingredient in the Mediterranean region. Containing eight essential amino acids, barley has been widely used in many cultures and has been proven to regulate blood sugar levels.

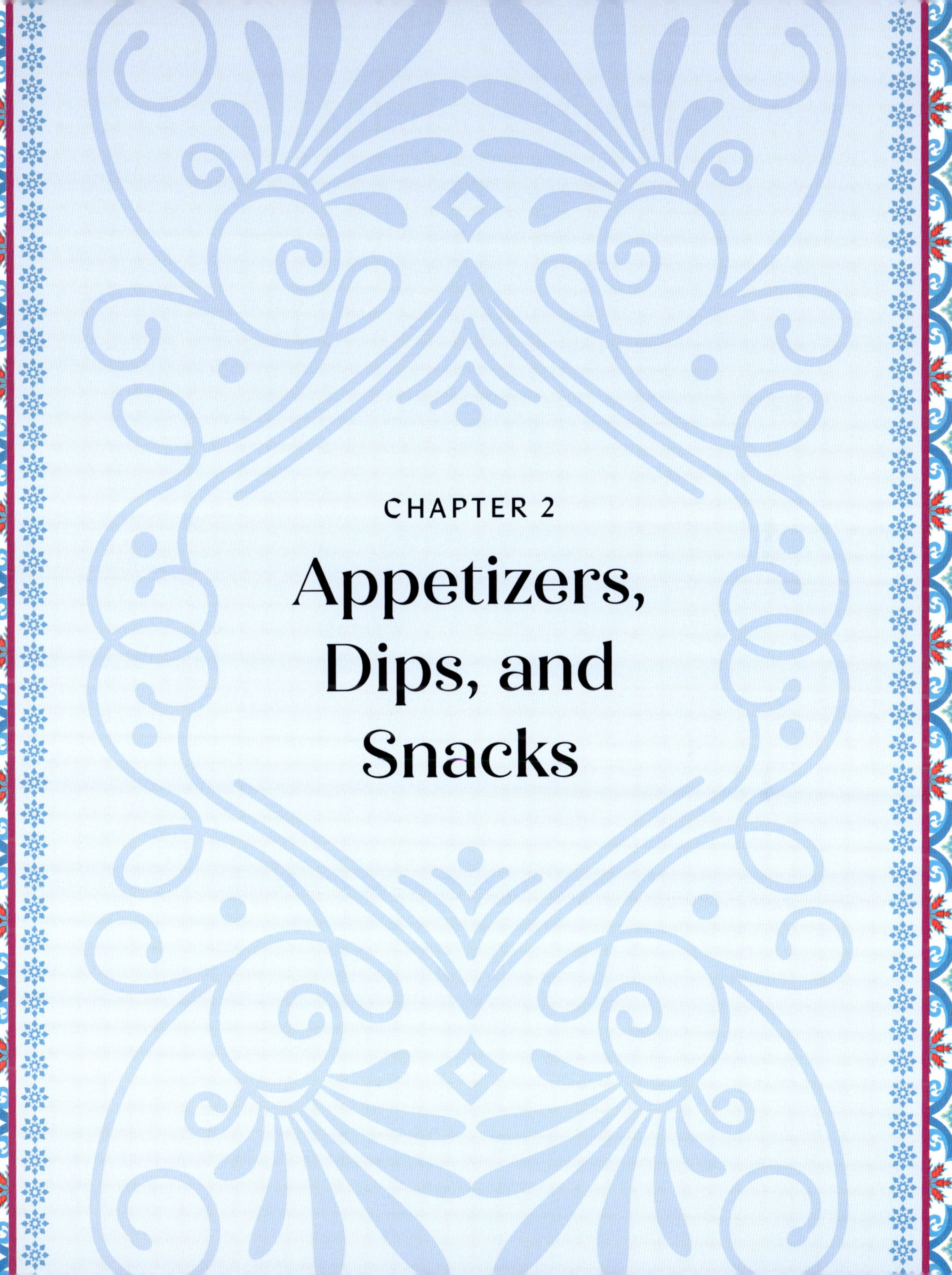

CHAPTER 2

Appetizers, Dips, and Snacks

Provençal Herb Tapenade

The Romans named Provence Provincia Romana, or The Roman Province, in Latin when Nice was their capital in the first century CE. The Romans left both vineyards and olive groves as well as the Latin language during their time there. As a result, Provençal cuisine developed strong Italian undertones, as this recipe demonstrates. The word *tapenade* comes from the ancient Provençal word *tapena*, which means "to cover." This citrusy olive paste makes the perfect topping for bread, crudités, vegetables, pasta, fish, and chicken.

TOTAL PREP AND COOK TIME: 15 minutes **YIELD:** About 1 cup (250 g)

¾ cup (96 g) pitted black olives (picholine or kalamata work well)

3 teaspoons (26 g) capers, rinsed and drained well

3 cloves garlic, chopped

⅓ cup (80 ml) extra-virgin olive oil, or to taste

1 teaspoon lemon zest

Freshly ground black pepper, to taste

1. Combine the olives, capers, and garlic in a food processor.
2. Remove the lid of the spout and slowly pour in the olive oil, a little at a time, while pulsing the food processor on and off. The tapenade should have a paste-like consistency, but should not be completely smooth.
3. Stir in the lemon zest and season with pepper.

Mediterranean Tradition

Reinventing leftovers into culinary creations is an art form so integral to the region, that it is taken for granted. Leftover roasted chicken or fish and raw vegetables taste great dipped into tapenade. You can stir it into blanched green beans tossed with cucumbers, chickpeas, and cherry tomatoes for a fun and flavorful salad.

PER SERVING: 45 CALORIES | 1 G CARBOHYDRATE (0 G FIBER | 0 G ADDED SUGARS | 1 G NET CARBS) | 0 G PROTEIN | 5 G FAT | 150 MG SODIUM

Fried Baby Potatoes in Allioli

This is a Spanish tapa from the Levantine coast of Alicante called *patatitas fritas con allioli*. It is a garlic-lover's dream dish.

TOTAL PREP AND COOK TIME: 60 minutes **YIELD:** 8 servings

4 large garlic cloves, peeled

½ teaspoon salt

1 medium egg

1 cup (250 ml) extra-virgin olive oil

1 pound (455 g) baby Yukon Gold potatoes, 1 inch (2.5 cm) in diameter or less, left unpeeled

6 cups (1.5 L) extra-virgin olive oil, for frying

Salt to taste

1. Prepare the allioli: In a mortar, mash the garlic and salt together with a pestle until mushy. Transfer the garlic to a food processor with the egg and process for 30 seconds. With the machine running, slowly drizzle in 1 cup (250 ml) oil in a very thin stream through the feed tube until absorbed. Cover with plastic wrap and refrigerate for 1 hour before using to let the emulsion solidify a bit.

2. Bring a medium-size saucepan of water to a boil and cook the potatoes until ever so slightly tender, about 5 minutes. Drain and dry thoroughly with paper towels.

3. Preheat the frying oil in a deep fryer or an 8-inch (20 cm) saucepan fitted with a basket insert to 375°F (180°C, or gas mark 4). Cook the whole potatoes in the 6 cups (1.5 L) hot oil until crisp, tender, and brown, about 8 minutes. Remove with a slotted spoon, drain on paper towels, season with salt, and serve with toothpicks with the allioli on the side.

PER SERVING: 440 CALORIES | 11 G CARBOHYDRATE (1 G FIBER | 0 G ADDED SUGARS | 10 G NET CARBS) | 2 G PROTEIN | 45 G FAT | 150 MG SODIUM

Kale and Almond Pesto Sauce

This is a quick and delicious uncooked sauce, perfect for busy evenings that require something delicious and nutritious. Up the nutrition factor on the traditional Basil Pesto by replacing the basil with kale and the pine nuts with almonds. The strong flavors work beautifully with healthful whole-wheat and gluten-free quinoa pastas while delivering extra vitamins and minerals. Try short cuts such as fusilli and farfalle for this sauce.

TOTAL PREP AND COOK TIME: 20 minutes **YIELD:** 6 servings (enough for 1 pound [455 g] of pasta)

¾ cup (175 ml) good-quality extra-virgin olive oil

3 cups (200 g) fresh baby kale

2 cloves garlic

¼ cup (36 g) whole almonds

¼ cup (25 g) freshly grated Parmigiano-Reggiano cheese

¼ cup (25 g) freshly grated Romano cheese

1. Place all of the ingredients except the cheese in a food processor.
2. Mix to combine and form a smooth paste.
3. Scoop the mixture out of food processor into a bowl. Stir in the cheese.

Mediterranean Tradition

Pesto sauce should never be heated. To freeze pesto, mix to combine all ingredients except the cheese, cover the top with additional olive oil, and place in an airtight container. Thaw overnight in the refrigerator before using. Pesto can also be stored in the refrigerator for up to 1 week.

PER SERVING: 320 CALORIES | 4 G CARBOHYDRATE (2 G FIBER | 0 G ADDED SUGARS | 3 G NET CARBS) | 5 G PROTEIN | 34 G FAT | 95 MG SODIUM

Tahini-Zucchini Dip

If you're all "hummused out" and want to wake up your taste buds, give this dip a try. The base of this dip is tahini, which is made of ground sesame seeds, plus zucchini to lighten it up a bit while adding a pop of color. You can even dip crispy sliced radishes or carrots into this, or serve it as a dip with chicken.

TOTAL PREP AND COOK TIME: 20 minutes **YIELD:** 8 servings (¼ cup [65 g] each)

1 clove garlic, peeled

1 medium zucchini, sliced

½ cup (130 g) tahini (sesame seed paste; see Recipe Note)

¼ cup (60 ml) lemon juice

½ teaspoon salt

1. In a food processor, mince the garlic.
2. Add the zucchini and process until finely chopped.
3. Add the tahini, lemon juice, and salt.
4. Process until smooth.

SUGGESTIONS AND VARIATIONS

Sprinkle ground sumac, a spice, on top for an added pop of color and intense lemony taste.

RECIPE NOTE

At grocery stores, you can find tahini in jars in the nut butter section or in cans in the international food section.

PER SERVING: 94 CALORIES | 4 G CARBOHYDRATE (4 G FIBER | 1 G ADDED SUGARS | 3 G NET CARBS) | 3 G PROTEIN | 8 G FAT | 152 MG SODIUM

Turkish Yogurt, Garlic, and Dill Sauce

Yogurt is one of the traditional pleasures of kitchens around the Mediterranean. It's usually enjoyed for breakfast, or a light snack, with fresh figs and luscious mountain honey. For best results, drain the yogurt overnight. After draining the yogurt, enjoy the excess liquid, or whey, as a refreshing drink. It is full of healthful probiotic nutrients, and good bacteria known to aid digestion.

TOTAL PREP AND COOK TIME: 30 minutes, plus drainage time **YIELD:** 8 servings

3 cups (690 g) plain organic full-fat yogurt

2 English cucumbers, peeled and diced

Unrefined sea salt or salt

¼ cup (16 g) fresh dill, chopped

1 clove garlic, minced

1 small yellow onion, grated and drained

1. Place the yogurt in a medium colander over a bowl to drain overnight in the refrigerator.
2. Place the cucumbers in a colander and sprinkle with ¼ teaspoon salt. Let stand for 20 minutes.
3. Rinse off the salt and add cucumbers to yogurt. Stir in the dill. Add the garlic and onion, and season with salt to taste.
4. Serve immediately to prevent salad from becoming runny. If storing, place in an airtight container in the refrigerator and drain off excess liquid before serving.

Mediterranean Tradition

This type of sauce is considered a salad in the region. It can be eaten with pita at breakfast time, or as a garnish for kabobs or grilled meats.

PER SERVING: 70 CALORIES | 7 G CARBOHYDRATE (1 G FIBER | 0 G ADDED SUGARS | 6 G NET CARBS) | 4 G PROTEIN | 3 G FAT | 45 MG SODIUM

Herb-Marinated Mozzarella

This Italian classic makes a tasty and beautiful appetizer or edible gift. Feel free to alter the recipe, using the herbs you have on hand. Garlic, capers, chopped olives, and hot peppers are all popular additions. You can also use larger pieces of mozzarella, instead of bocconcini, and slice them into ¼-inch (6 mm) slices.

TOTAL PREP AND COOK TIME: 1 hour **YIELD:** 4 servings

¼ cup (60 ml) good-quality, extra-virgin olive oil

3 teaspoons (7.5 g) mixed fresh herbs, such as finely chopped fresh flat-leaf parsley, finely chopped fresh basil, and finely chopped fresh oregano

¼ teaspoon crushed red pepper flakes

¼ teaspoon unrefined sea salt or salt

Pinch of freshly ground black pepper

1 pound (455 g) fresh bocconcini mozzarella balls, preferably from buffalo milk

Olives and crackers or bread to serve

1. In a small bowl, combine the oil, herbs, red pepper flakes, salt, and pepper.
2. Place the mozzarella balls in a shallow bowl. Drizzle the oil and herb mixture over mozzarella. Let stand for an hour. Serve with olives and crackers or bread.

Mediterranean Tradition

Buffalos were introduced to the Campania region of Italy via Egypt in antiquity. Their rich, sweet milk has been used to produce deeply flavored butter and cheese ever since. These mozzarella balls are a great stir-in to pastas and salads when the temperature is too high to spend a long time in the kitchen. If buffalo-milk mozzarella is not available in your area, look for the freshest variety possible.

PER SERVING: 174 CALORIES | 1 G CARBOHYDRATE (0 G FIBER | 0 G ADDED SUGARS | 1 G NET CARBS) | 12 G PROTEIN | 10 G FAT | 245 MG SODIUM

Crispy Roasted Chickpeas

These are the perfect antidote to a crunchy, salty snack craving, plus you're getting protein, fiber, iron, and the goodness of beans. These crisp chickpeas can also be enjoyed over salads, soups, and cottage cheese, adding texture.

TOTAL PREP AND COOK TIME: 50 minutes **YIELD:** 4 servings, ¼ cup (100 g) each

1 can (15-ounce [425 g]) chickpeas, drained and rinsed well

2 tablespoons (30 ml) extra-virgin olive oil

¼ teaspoon kosher salt

Freshly ground black pepper, to taste

1 teaspoon ground sumac

1. Preheat the oven to 350°F (180°C, or gas mark 4) convection (if available). Line a baking sheet with parchment paper.
2. After draining and rinsing the chickpeas, pour them onto a clean towel and move the towel back and forth on the countertop to dry the chickpeas. This thorough drying helps crisp the chickpeas during baking.
3. Place the chickpeas on the prepared baking sheet and drizzle with the olive oil. Sprinkle with the salt and pepper. Roast until golden and crispy, about 40 minutes. Sprinkle with the sumac. Allow them to cool completely before sealing them in a container. The longer they can sit uncovered and dry out, the better.

SUGGESTIONS AND VARIATIONS

Feel free to play around with different spices on these, like turmeric, curry powder, cumin, and chili powder.

PER SERVING: 120 CALORIES | 9 G CARBOHYDRATE (3 G FIBER | 0 G ADDED SUGARS | 6 G NET CARBS) | 3 G PROTEIN | 8 G FAT | 189 MG SODIUM

Homemade Yogurt Cheese

It's surprisingly simple to make Lebanon's namesake yogurt cheese. Since there are only a few ingredients in this recipe, quality ingredients are paramount. Choose the best-quality yogurt you can find, preferably one made of sheep and goat's milk cheese from a Mediterranean import store. Try drizzling with unfiltered olive oil, if possible. You can also add finely diced celery, radishes, carrots, or tomatoes to your labneh. Be sure to save the strained liquid—it contains all of the healthful probiotics from the yogurt and makes a great addition to smoothies.

TOTAL PREP AND COOK TIME: 15 minutes, plus refrigeration time **YIELD:** About 2 cups

4 cups (920 g) full-fat plain yogurt

1 teaspoon unrefined sea salt or salt

Good-quality, extra-virgin olive oil, unfiltered, if possible

Za'atar

6 to 8 black olives

Whole-Wheat Pita Bread (page 18) or other bread, for serving

1. Line a nonreactive strainer with a few layers of cheesecloth and set it over a deep bowl, one deep enough so that the bottom of the strainer is 2 to 3 inches (5 to 7.5 cm) above the bottom of the bowl where the strained liquid (whey) will collect.
2. Stir the salt into the yogurt. Using a spatula, scrape the yogurt into the lined strainer. Fold the ends of the cheesecloth over the yogurt and refrigerate overnight, or for a minimum of 12 hours.
3. Remove the thickened strained cheese (labneh) from the cloth. Transfer the mixture to a shallow serving dish and smooth out the top in a circular fashion using a spatula. Make a few swirls in the labneh, then drizzle a fairly generous amount of olive oil in the indentations. Sprinkle with za'atar, garnish with the olives in the middle, and serve with bread for dipping.

Mediterranean Tradition

The word Lebanon *is derived from the word* labneh, *which comes from the Arabic word for milk,* laban. Za'atar *is the Arabic word for a variety of wild thyme. It is also the name of a spice mix, such as what is called for in this recipe, containing wild thyme, coriander, sesame seeds, Middle Eastern sumac, and sea salt.*

PER SERVING: 40 CALORIES | 3 G CARBOHYDRATE (0 G FIBER | 0 G ADDED SUGARS | 3 G NET CARBS) | 2 G PROTEIN | 2 G FAT | 190 MG SODIUM

Cucumber Cups with Lobster Salad

This is a cucumber version of croûtes made with bread. This Provençal preparation is quite nice because the rich taste of lobster is suited to the light, watery cucumber.

TOTAL PREP AND COOK TIME: 30 minutes

YIELD: 18 cups, 10 servings

One 1⅓-pounds (605 g) live lobster

¼ cup mayonnaise, preferably homemade (below)

Salt and freshly ground white pepper, to taste

⅛ to ¼ teaspoon hot Hungarian paprika, to taste

2 large cucumbers, tiny portion of the ends trimmed, peeled, and cut into 1-inch-thick rounds (18 or so rounds total)

18 small fresh parsley leaves

1. Bring a large pot filled with an inch of water to a boil and cook the lobster until bright red, about 15 minutes.
2. Drain, let cool, crack all the shells, and remove the meat and any tomalley and coral.
3. Once the lobster is cool, chop and mix it with the mayonnaise and salt, pepper, and paprika to taste.
4. With a melon baller, scoop out the center of the cucumber slices to create a small well, making sure you don't cut through the bottom or sides. Stuff the lobster mixture into the cucumbers, garnish the top of each with a parsley leaf, and refrigerate until needed.

PER SERVING: 70 CALORIES | 2 G CARBOHYDRATE (0 G FIBER | 0 G ADDED SUGARS | 2 G NET CARBS) | 4 G PROTEIN | 4.5 G FAT | 120 MG SODIUM

Shrimp and Lemon Canapés

In Provence, a canapé such as this one could also be garnished with a caper.

TOTAL PREP AND COOK TIME: 30 minutes

YIELD: 60 canapés, 20 servings

Sixty ¼-inch-thick slices French baguette

¼ cup (60 g) mayonnaise

¾ pound (340 g) very small peeled cooked shrimp

16 very thin slices Meyer lemon, each cut into eight triangles, leaving the peel on

Salt, to taste

1. Spread the bread slices with the mayonnaise.
2. Place some shrimp on top and flank with 2 triangles of the sliced lemon.
3. Season with salt and serve or refrigerate.

Antipasto from Italy

An antipasto is not the course before the pasta, but rather it means the food served before the meal, pasto. Historically, appetizers—that is, antipasti—did not play a very important part in the regional cooking of the Italian peninsula, unlike other European countries, especially France. Antipasti were nonexistent in the south and were always more evident in the cuisines of the north.

PER SERVING: 140 CALORIES | 23 G CARBOHYDRATE (0 G FIBER | 1 G ADDED SUGARS | 22 G NET CARBS) | 5 G PROTEIN | 2 G FAT | 350 MG SODIUM

Shrimp and Garlic

One of the most charming restaurants in Granada is the Sevilla Restaurant by the cathedral. The outdoor seating has a lovely, shaded view of a portal of the cathedral. The restaurant serves gambas al ajillo, the famous Andalusian tapa shrimp and garlic, but it may seem disappointing when you first see it. The earthenware casserole it comes in is pathetically small, and it is a relatively inexpensive item. But one taste will leave you closing your eyes in ecstasy and slowing down. The bowl is a bit deeper than you may expect, so there are about twenty delicately cooked hidden shrimp that are so fresh they literally melt in your mouth. They are submerged in a liquid that is a very garlicky hot sauce—colored with paprika and washed in olive oil. You can use your bread to dunk into this powerful garlic sauce, noticing that there are sliced garlic and little black pine nut–sized hot chiles, which have some kind of almost Asian taste to them.

TOTAL PREP AND COOK TIME: 20 minutes **YIELD:** 8 servings

4 pounds (1.8 kg) fresh large shrimp with their heads or 2 pounds (910 g) previously frozen headless shrimp, shells and/or heads removed and saved for shrimp stock, if desired

2 tablespoons (30 g) coarse sea salt

2 cups (500 ml) extra-virgin olive oil

8 to 10 large garlic cloves, sliced

20 very small Thai chiles (also called chili pequín or pequín)

2 teaspoons hot Spanish paprika

1. Dry the shrimp with paper towels. Place them in a bowl, sprinkle with the salt, and leave for 10 minutes.
2. In an 8- to 10-inch earthenware casserole (preferably, or other stovetop-proof casserole), heat the olive oil over medium-high heat.
3. Once the oil is smoking, add the garlic and chiles and cook until the garlic starts to turn color, 30 to 60 seconds, then add the shrimp and paprika and cook until orange-red, 3 to 4 minutes.
4. Serve immediately from the casserole with lots of crusty Italian or French bread.

PER SERVING: 660 CALORIES | 3 G CARBOHYDRATE (0 G FIBER | 0 G ADDED SUGARS | 3 G NET CARBS) | 31 G PROTEIN | 58 G FAT | 3050 MG SODIUM

Puff Pastry of Swiss Chard and Onion

This recipe from Ajaccio on the island of Corsica is called bastella. It is exceedingly simple, and on the face of it doesn't look like it would be tasty, but it is—very much so. The Swiss chard is cooked in olive oil with sliced onions, then stuffed inside rectangles of puff pastry before being baked. Some Corsican cooks also add ground beef or veal to the stuffing. There may be a long and twisted history to the Corsican bastella. If using frozen puff pastry, defrost according to package instructions.

TOTAL PREP AND COOK TIME: 50 minutes **YIELD:** 12 pastries, 12 servings

3 tablespoons (45 ml) extra-virgin olive oil

1 medium-size onion, very thinly sliced

1½ pounds (680 g) Swiss chard, white stems removed, leaves washed well, dried well, and chopped

Salt and freshly ground black pepper, to taste

¾ pound (340 g) store-bought puff pastry

1. In a large skillet, heat the olive oil over medium-high heat, then cook the onion until soft, about 4 minutes, stirring. Add the Swiss chard and cook until it wilts, about 5 minutes, stirring. Season with salt and pepper.
2. Preheat the oven to 400°F (200°C).
3. Roll the puff pastry out slightly on a lightly floured work surface so it forms a 14-inch (35 cm) square. Cut into 12 squares and evenly divide the stuffing among the squares, placing some in the center of each. Fold the puff pastry over to form a rectangle, crimp the edges together with the tines of a fork, and arrange on a baking sheet.
4. Bake until golden, about 25 minutes. Serve warm or hot.

PER SERVING: 200 CALORIES | 16 G CARBOHYDRATE (0 G FIBER | 0 G ADDED SUGARS | 14 G NET CARBS) | 2 G PROTEIN | 15 G FAT | 100 MG SODIUM

Pizza-Style Frittata

This Italian frittata is called *frittata alla pizzaiola*, which means something like "à la pizza style," because it is meant to resemble a pizza. The frittata is finished under the broiler and when the sides puff up, it will look like a pizza with an inviting golden crust. If you don't have a skillet that can go under a broiler, use whatever skillet you have and let the handle stick out, with the oven or broiler door open.

TOTAL PREP AND COOK TIME: 20 minutes	YIELD: 4 servings

1½ tablespoons (21 g) unsalted butter

1 tablespoon (15 ml) extra-virgin olive oil

4 large eggs, beaten

½ teaspoon salt

4 large, thin slices ripe tomato

6 imported black olives, pitted and chopped

6 thin slices Fontina Val d'Aosta or provolone cheese

1 tablespoon (2.5 g) finely chopped fresh parsley leaves

1. Preheat the broiler.
2. In a 10-inch (25 cm) ovenproof nonstick skillet, melt the butter with the olive oil over medium heat until the butter begins to turn light brown. Pour the eggs into the skillet, season with the salt, and quickly arrange the tomato slices on top, along with the olives sprinkled around. Cover with the cheese and sprinkle on the parsley.
3. Place the skillet under the broiler and broil until the top sets, is lightly speckled with brown spots, and the edges have puffed up. Serve immediately, cut into wedges.

Of Frittatas and Omelettes

A frittata is different from an omelette in that it is made like a pancake. The beaten eggs are poured into a pan and cooked on one side, then the frittata is covered, placed in an oven, or flipped to be finished. The frittata is then eaten cold or hot, usually as a light lunch dish or as an antipasto. An omelette, on the other hand, is cooked in a pan and folded over onto itself, stuffed or not, to form a puffy, soft cylinder. It is always eaten hot.

PER SERVING: 191 CALORIES,1 G CARBOHYDRATE (0 G FIBER | 0 G ADDED SUGARS | 1 G NET CARBS) | 15 G PROTEIN | 8 G FAT | 288 MG SODIUM

Mussels with Feta Cheese

Theo Tsakkis and his wife Constance are the owners of Nireas, a restaurant serving traditional food from Rhodes, which is a rarity on the tourist-infested island. The old town of Rhodes is a walled city that will make you feel you're about to encounter one of the Knights Templar at any moment. Theo makes this wonderful dish of mussels and feta called midye saganaki.

TOTAL PREP AND COOK TIME: 50 minutes **YIELD:** 8 servings

4 pounds (1.8 kg) mussels, scrubbed and debearded (see below)

¼ cup (60 ml) water

6 tablespoons (90 ml) extra-virgin olive oil

2 medium-size onions, chopped

2 green bell peppers, seeded and chopped

¾ pound (340 g) ripe tomatoes, cut in half, seeds squeezed out, grated against the largest holes of a grater, and skins discarded

¼ pound (115 g) imported Greek or Bulgarian feta cheese, cut into small cubes

1. Place the cleaned mussels in a pot with the water, cover, and turn the heat to high. Remove the mussels as soon as they open, 6 to 9 minutes. Discard any mussels that remain firmly shut. Remove the mussels from their shells and set aside.

2. In a medium-size skillet, heat the olive oil over medium-high heat, then cook the onions and peppers until the onions are translucent, about 8 minutes, stirring occasionally. Add the tomatoes and cook until most of the liquid has evaporated, about 5 minutes.

3. Add the mussels and scatter the cubes of cheese around the skillet evenly. Cook until the cheese melts a bit and the food is hot, about 8 minutes, then serve hot right from the skillet with crusty bread.

DEBEARDING

Nearly all the mussels you will encounter in the market today are cultivated mussels. They will usually be rather well cleaned for you already, but it's a good idea to give them a cleaning in fresh cold water. They will have a little string of what looks like seaweed hanging off their hinge by which they attach themselves to rocks. This "beard," called a byssus, must be pulled off.

PER SERVING: 310 CALORIES | 12 G CARBOHYDRATE (1 G FIBER | 0 G ADDED SUGARS | 10 G NET CARBS) | 28 G PROTEIN | 18 G FAT | 930 MG SODIUM

CHAPTER 3

Soups and Salads

Cream of Asparagus Soup

Asparagus soup is a classic first course in Spain. Served in clear glasses or little mugs, it makes a delicious and elegant starter. This soup is simple to make, and it reheats well.

TOTAL PREP AND COOK TIME: 25 minutes **YIELD:** 4 servings

2 pounds (910 g) asparagus, cleaned and trimmed

2 cups (475 ml) whole milk

2 cups (475 ml) water

¼ teaspoon unrefined sea salt or salt

Freshly ground black pepper, to taste

4 tablespoons (16 g) parsley, finely chopped

1. Place the asparagus, milk, and water in a large saucepan. Add salt and pepper, and stir. Bring to a boil over high heat. Stir, reduce heat to medium-low, and simmer, uncovered, for 8 to 10 minutes, or until asparagus is tender.
2. Pour the soup into a blender. Remove the center spout from the lid to prevent it from bursting. Place the lid on the blender, and hold a kitchen towel over the center hole. Purée soup until it is blended. Whip the soup for 1 minute more and return it to the saucepan.
3. Heat the soup on low until warm. Taste and adjust seasonings, if necessary. Pour into clear glasses or coffee mugs, and top with parsley.

Mediterranean Tradition

When asparagus is bountiful during the spring in the northern Mediterranean region, it is transformed into a multitude of delicious dishes. Asparagus is packed with vitamins and minerals, which prevent many forms of cancer and heart disease.

PER SERVING: 120 CALORIES | 15 G CARBOHYDRATE (5 G FIBER | 0 G ADDED SUGARS | 10 G NET CARBS) | 9 G PROTEIN | 4.5 G FAT | 210 MG SODIUM

Quinoa, Arugula, and Fig Salad

This French spin on tabbouleh replaces bulgur wheat with nutritious quinoa—the ancient grain that supplies all nine essential amino acids, making it a complete protein! If fresh figs are not in season, substitute pears, apples, oranges, or the fruit of your choice. In addition to being used in this salad, cooked quinoa tastes great at breakfast with fruit, cinnamon, chopped nuts, and milk.

TOTAL PREP AND COOK TIME: 25 minutes **YIELD:** 4 servings as a vegetarian main, or 8 as a side dish

1 cup (185 g) dry quinoa, rinsed

½ cup (118 ml) extra-virgin olive oil

Juice of 1 lemon

¼ teaspoon unrefined sea salt or salt

Freshly ground black pepper, to taste

1 pint (228 g) fresh figs, quartered

11 ounces (312 g) baby arugula

1. Bring 2 cups (475 ml) of water to a boil in a medium saucepan over high heat. Add the quinoa, stir, reduce heat to low, and cover. Allow to simmer until all liquid is absorbed, 10 to 15 minutes. Remove from the stove and allow to cool completely.
2. Whisk the olive oil, lemon juice, salt, and black pepper together to form a vinaigrette.
3. Place the quinoa in a large bowl and lightly fluff with a fork. Combine with the vinaigrette. Gently stir in the figs. Place the arugula on a platter. Pour the quinoa mixture over the arugula and serve.

Mediterranean Tradition

A new trend in the Mediterranean region is to use quinoa instead of rice in traditional recipes. Try adding cooked quinoa to soups, beans, and stews to increase their nutritional value. You can also use cooked quinoa as a bed for main courses. A terrific variation on this salad substitutes the juice of 1 orange for the lemon, and 2 cups (454 g) fresh berries and 11 ounces (312 g) baby spinach for the figs and arugula.

Provençal Bistro Carrot Salad

This is a French bistro classic—simple to prepare, and perfect as a light side dish.

TOTAL PREP AND COOK TIME: 15 minutes | **YIELD:** 4 servings

6 tablespoons (90 ml) lemon-mustard vinaigrette, store-bought or homemade

5 medium carrots, peeled, trimmed, and grated

Unrefined sea salt or salt, to taste

Freshly ground black pepper, to taste

¼ cup (15 g) finely chopped parsley

4 leaves Bibb lettuce, for serving

1 ripe tomato, quartered

1. In a small bowl, whisk the vinaigrette so that it is evenly distributed and emulsified.
2. Add the carrots, and season with salt and pepper.
3. Toss in parsley and mix well.
4. Serve garnished with Bibb lettuce and tomato wedges.

Mediterranean Tradition

Sometimes a variety of simple, already-assembled salads like this one are displayed beautifully at salad bars in restaurants in the region. Patrons of the salad bar select from a dazzling array of salads already created for them. This style can be adapted to your home kitchen. You can make up salads (without the dressings) in advance, store them in airtight containers, and enjoy a scoop of each for a quick and nutritious lunch or dinner.

PER SERVING: 160 CALORIES | 12 G CARBOHYDRATE (3 G FIBER | 2 G ADDED SUGARS | 9 G NET CARBS) | 1 G PROTEIN | 12 G FAT | 230 MG SODIUM

Cypriot Halloumi, Watermelon, and Basil Kabobs

Halloumi is a soft, salty cheese with herbal undertones that has been crafted on the island of Cyprus since antiquity. Artisan Halloumi cheese is still made of sheep and goat's milk the way it was millennia ago. On the island of Cyprus, watermelon is paired with feta cheese for a sweet and salty combination that can't be beat. It's the perfect after-dinner treat to enjoy with friends on a balmy evening.

TOTAL PREP AND COOK TIME: 15 minutes **YIELD:** 8 servings

2 cups (300 g) watermelon cubes (1 inch, or 2.5 cm)

1 pound (455 g) Halloumi cheese, cut into 1-inch (2.5 cm) cubes

1 bunch fresh basil

¼ cup (60 ml) good-quality extra-virgin olive oil

Short wooden skewers, for serving

1. Thread a piece of watermelon onto a skewer. Follow with a piece of Halloumi and a basil leaf.
2. Continue until all of the watermelon and Halloumi have been used up.
3. Drizzle with olive oil.

Mediterranean Tradition

The base of the Mediterranean Diet Pyramid emphasizes eating meals with others, and Cyprus is the perfect place to do it! Local tavernas offer dozens (often as many as fifty-four) of mezedes, or small plates, to groups of friends who spend hours at the table slowly savoring the delicious treats.

PER SERVING: 260 CALORIES | 3 G CARBOHYDRATE (0 G FIBER | 0 G ADDED SUGARS | 3 G NET CARBS) | 12 G PROTEIN | 23 G FAT | 600 MG SODIUM

Pomegranate, Lentil, and Mixed Green Salad

This salad combines protein-packed lentils with sweet and tart pomegranate seeds and crunchy mixed greens for a sweet and savory combination that tastes as good as it is healthy.

TOTAL PREP AND COOK TIME: 50 minutes **YIELD:** 4 servings

½ cup (96 g) lentils, rinsed, drained, and sorted

1 bay leaf

4 cups (120 g) mixed field greens or baby spinach

¼ cup (45 g) pomegranate arils (seeds)

¼ cup (60 ml) pomegranate juice

2 tablespoons (30 ml) extra-virgin olive oil

Unrefined sea salt or salt, to taste

Freshly ground black pepper, to taste

1. Place the lentils in a medium saucepan and cover with water. Bring to a boil over high heat, reduce heat to low, and add the bay leaf. Simmer, uncovered, for 30 minutes, or until tender. Drain, and discard the bay leaf.
2. Divide the mixed greens evenly among 4 salad plates. Sprinkle pomegranate arils over the greens.
3. Heat the pomegranate juice in a small saucepan over medium-high heat until it boils. Reduce heat to low and simmer for 5 to 10 minutes, until thick and syrupy.
4. Slowly pour in the olive oil while whisking vigorously to form a homogenous dressing. Taste and season with salt and pepper as needed. Sprinkle lentils evenly over the salad and drizzle dressing over the top.

Mediterranean Tradition

Try preparing lentils in large batches in advance so that they will be on hand and can easily be incorporated into recipes when needed.

PER SERVING: 170 CALORIES | 24 G CARBOHYDRATE (3 G FIBER | 0 G ADDED SUGARS | 21 G NET CARBS) | 7 G PROTEIN | 8 G FAT | 20 MG SODIUM

Breakfast Salad

The key to this is cooking the eggs just until the whites are done, but with the yolks still runny, since that becomes the dressing. Try using a trusty microwave egg poacher, which cooks eggs close to perfectly in under 1 minute.

TOTAL PREP AND COOK TIME: 10 minutes **YIELD:** 1 serving

1 large egg (or 2 if you are extra hungry)

2 cups (60 g) baby arugula or spinach

⅓ large avocado, peeled, pitted, and diced

Juice of 1 lemon wedge

Pinch of salt

Freshly ground black pepper, to taste

1. Cook the eggs with your preferred method—either sunny-side up or poached—with the yolks still runny.
2. Place the arugula, avocado, lemon juice, salt, and pepper in a mixing bowl. Add the eggs, breaking them up so the yolk releases. Toss.

SUGGESTIONS AND VARIATIONS

You can certainly embellish this salad with other ingredients you have on hand, like cherry tomatoes and leftover bits of protein from dinner, such as beans or chopped pieces of meat.

PER SERVING: 150 CALORIES | 7 G CARBOHYDRATE (4 G FIBER | 0 G ADDED SUGARS | 3 G NET CARBS) | 8 G PROTEIN | 11 G FAT | 232 MG SODIUM

Middle Eastern Cottage Cheese, Vegetable, and Olive Salad

This healthy salad is eaten for breakfast in Egypt and other places in the eastern Mediterranean.

TOTAL PREP AND COOK TIME: 20 minutes **YIELD:** 6 servings

3 cups (675 g) small curd cottage cheese

1 tomato, chopped

1 baby (Persian) cucumber, or ⅓ English cucumber, diced

¼ cup (32 g) kalamata olives, pitted and chopped

Unrefined sea salt or salt, to taste

Freshly ground black pepper, to taste

¼ cup (60 ml) extra-virgin olive oil (unfiltered if possible)

¼ cup (15 g) chopped fresh parsley

6 pieces Whole-Wheat Pita Bread, quartered (see page 18)

or

Raw vegetables for serving

1. Combine the cottage cheese, tomato, cucumber, and olives in a medium bowl. Toss gently to combine. Taste, and season with salt and pepper, if needed.

2. Place the cottage cheese on a dinner plate, and using a spatula, smooth out the top. Drizzle olive oil on the top and garnish with parsley. Serve with pita wedges or crudités.

Mediterranean Tradition

Savory breakfasts are a way that many North African and Eastern European communities start their day. It's great when you're in the mood for a Mediterranean-inspired brunch or vegetarian meal.

PER SERVING: 470 CALORIES | 59 G CARBOHYDRATE (6 G FIBER | 1 G ADDED SUGARS | 52 G NET CARBS) | 21 G PROTEIN | 19 G FAT | 1140 MG SODIUM

Cucumber Yogurt Salad

Leben can be as much a staple in homes as ketchup is. You can make it by simmering whole milk until it is "so hot that you can't hold your pinky finger in it," followed by squeezing the liquid from the curd while wrapped in cheesecloth. However, this recipe uses a shortcut that you may appreciate—head straight for the store-bought Greek yogurt! To make it extra rich and delicious, you can use 2% or whole-milk yogurt, rather than nonfat yogurt.

TOTAL PREP AND COOK TIME: 15 minutes | **YIELD:** 5 servings, ¼ cup (60 g) each

1 medium cucumber, peeled and sliced into half-moons (1¾ cups [210 g])

½ cup (115 g) 2% plain Greek yogurt, pouring off any liquid from the top

1 scallion, thinly sliced

2 teaspoons white wine vinegar

½ teaspoon salt

1. Combine all of the ingredients in a bowl. You may enjoy the salad immediately or chill until ready to serve, pouring off any liquid.

RECIPE NOTE

A hard-core purist would salt the cucumbers first, let them sit for 30 minutes, then pat off the liquid released. But if you're hungry and want things ready instantly, you can pull the salad from the fridge. However, make sure you drain off the excess liquid first. But if you'd like to go the purist route, wait to add more salt to the salad until you've tasted it first.

PER SERVING: 24 CALORIES | 2 G CARBOHYDRATE (0 G FIBER | 0 G ADDED SUGARS | 2 G NET CARBS) | 3 G PROTEIN | 1 G FAT | 242 MG SODIUM

Tomato and Avocado Salad

As most people know, Andalusia is the home of gazpacho, but it is also the home of other tomato dishes that are just as satisfying, such as this pretty salad called *ensalada de tomates*, which can be served as a tapa, too. If you can find a variety of different tomatoes, such as orange cherry tomatoes and teardrop tomatoes, to throw in, it makes the salad all the more attractive. Do not refrigerate, and make the salad about 30 minutes before serving at the earliest.

TOTAL PREP AND COOK TIME: 20 minutes **YIELD:** 4 servings

1½ pounds (680 g) ripe tomatoes, different varieties and colors

1 ripe avocado, peeled, pitted, and diced or sliced

1 small garlic clove, finely chopped

1 tablespoon (2.5 g) finely chopped fresh basil leaves

Salt and freshly ground black pepper, to taste

½ teaspoon sugar

Extra-virgin olive oil

Very good-quality Spanish sherry vinegar

1. Trim the tomatoes and cut the larger ones and cherry tomatoes, if using, in half. Squeeze out the seeds.
2. Gently toss the tomatoes with the avocado and garlic in a serving bowl. Sprinkle on the basil, salt, pepper, and sugar. Drizzle with olive oil and vinegar to taste and toss gently again. Serve.

PER SERVING: 90 CALORIES | 11 G CARBOHYDRATE (4 G FIBER | 1 G ADDED SUGARS | 6 G NET CARBS) | 2 G PROTEIN | 6 G FAT | 10 MG SODIUM

Green Salad with Tomatoes, Cucumbers, and Lemon-Mint Vinaigrette

This salad is a staple served at Lebanese family gatherings. The light acidity of this salad balances perfectly with meats, dips, and seafood. Toss only the amount of salad you'll need in one sitting with the vinaigrette, to maintain crispness.

TOTAL PREP AND COOK TIME: 20 minutes **YIELD:** 4 servings, 1 cup (60 g) each (with 1 teaspoon vinaigrette)

¼ cup (60 ml) lemon-mint vinaigrette, store-bought or homemade 4 to 5 cups (220 to 275 g) torn or chopped Bibb or romaine lettuce (or use an Italian blend mix)

1 medium tomato, diced or sliced and quartered

½ medium cucumber, peeled, halved lengthwise, and sliced (about ¾ cup [89 g])

Salt and freshly ground black pepper, to taste

1. Whisk the vinaigrette in a small bowl until it is evenly distributed and emulsified.
2. To make the salad: In a bowl, combine the lettuce, tomato, and cucumber. Drizzle the dressing over the greens. Season with salt and pepper. Toss evenly and gently.

RECIPE NOTE

The vinaigrette makes enough for about two extra servings of salad. Therefore, you can either bulk up the salad recipe a bit or reserve the vinaigrette for other dishes, like seafood.

PER SERVING: 80 CALORIES | 4 G CARBOHYDRATE (2 G FIBER | 0 G ADDED SUGARS | 2 G NET CARBS) | 1 G PROTEIN | 7 G FAT | 80 MG SODIUM

Kale Salad with Blueberries and Feta

Kale and blueberries may seem like an unlikely pairing, but it works! The key to tender kale is to massage the vinaigrette into the greens and allow it to sit before enjoying. You can mix the entire batch and enjoy for the next couple of days, reserving the walnuts until ready to eat, to preserve crunchiness.

TOTAL PREP AND COOK TIME: 20 minutes   **YIELD:** 4 servings, 1 cup (80 g) each

½ cup (60 g) walnuts, chopped

1 (5-ounce [142 g]) bag kale

¼ teaspoon salt

3 tablespoons (45 ml) red wine vinaigrette, store-bought or homemade

1 tablespoon (14 g) mayonnaise

Freshly ground black pepper, to taste

½ cup (75 g) crumbled feta cheese

½ pint blueberries (about 1 cup [145 g])

1. Toast the walnuts in a sauté pan over medium heat until aromatic and golden, stirring frequently, about 7 minutes.
2. Place the kale in a medium-size bowl. Sprinkle with the salt.
3. Add the vinaigrette, mayonnaise, and pepper and toss thoroughly with tongs. Sprinkle in the feta and walnuts and toss. Sprinkle in the blueberries and toss gently with a spoon.

PER SERVING: 248 CALORIES | 9 G CARBOHYDRATE (3 G FIBER | 0 G ADDED SUGARS | 6 G NET CARBS) | 22 G PROTEIN | 400 G FAT | 400 MG SODIUM

Tuna Avocado Salad

The simplicity of cracking open a can of tuna, adding a few seasonings, and calling it lunch, especially in the summer, is unbeatable. For a richer taste, buy canned tuna in olive oil. You can create all sorts of different lunch plates with this protein-rich centerpiece. Pair with arugula, tomatoes, a sprinkle of chickpeas, toasted nuts, chopped herbs like parsley or basil, olives, or capers. Or all of the above if you're extra hungry!

TOTAL PREP AND COOK TIME: 10 minutes | **YIELD:** 1 serving

1 (5-ounce [142 g]) can tuna, drained well

⅓ large ripe avocado, peeled, pitted, and diced

1 tablespoon (15 ml) extra-virgin olive oil

1½ teaspoons balsamic vinegar

⅛ teaspoon garlic powder

⅛ teaspoon onion powder

⅛ teaspoon salt

Freshly ground black pepper, to taste

1. Break up the tuna in a bowl with a fork.
2. Add the remaining ingredients and stir.

PER SERVING: 306 CALORIES | 5 G CARBOHYDRATE (3 G FIBER | 0 G ADDED SUGARS | 2 G NET CARBS) | 25 G PROTEIN | 21 G FAT | 600 MG SODIUM

Salmon Salad with Dill, Capers, and Artichokes

If you enjoy canned salmon, you will love having this lunchtime salad over greens, with vegetable crudités, or in a lettuce wrap.

TOTAL PREP AND COOK TIME: 20 minutes | **YIELD:** 4 servings, about ¾ cup (175 g) each

1 (14.75-ounce [418 g]) can salmon, drained well

1 (14-ounce [396 g]) can quartered artichoke hearts, drained

¼ cup (60 ml) extra-virgin olive oil

3 tablespoons (45 ml) red wine vinegar

1 tablespoon (7.5 g) capers

½ teaspoon dried dill

¼ teaspoon salt

Freshly ground black pepper, to taste

1. In a mixing bowl, break up the salmon into smaller bits with a fork. Trim any tough outer tips from the artichokes, then cut the hearts into bite-size pieces.
2. Combine all of the ingredients in the bowl. You may enjoy right away or cover and chill until ready to serve. This salad keeps nicely for up to 5 days in the refrigerator.

RECIPE NOTE

You can peel away the skin of the salmon first. However, you can leave in the bones, which are edible and crumbly in canned salmon, and contribute a significant amount of calcium, too.

The outer tips of the artichoke leaves can be a bit tough and fibrous, even in canned artichokes, so you can trim those off.

PER SERVING: 292 CALORIES | 5 G CARBOHYDRATE (3 G FIBER | 0 G ADDED SUGARS | 26 G NET CARBS) | 19 G PROTEIN | 710 G FAT | 1,260 MG SODIUM

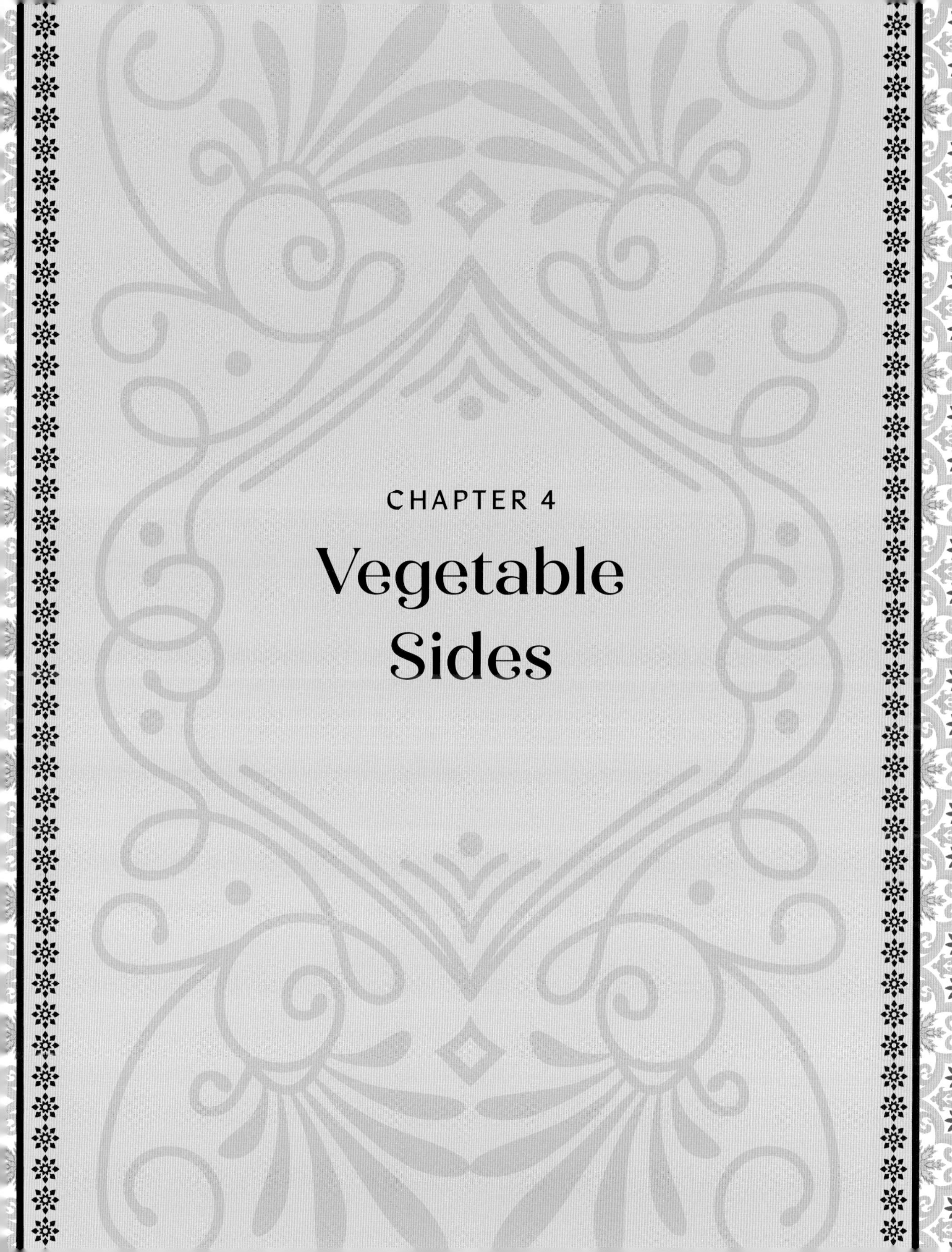

CHAPTER 4

Vegetable Sides

Roasted Brussels Sprouts with Herbes de Provence

If your only memories of Brussels sprouts are the boiled ones you grew up with, please allow this recipe to help you make new memories. Crispy Brussels sprouts on restaurant menus are all the rage. You can easily make them at home, too, but without the bacon fat.

TOTAL PREP AND COOK TIME: 30 minutes | **YIELD:** 4 servings

1 pound (455 g) Brussels sprouts, washed, stems cut off, outer leaves peeled if needed, then quartered

2 tablespoons (30 ml) extra-virgin olive oil

½ teaspoon herbes de Provence (or Italian seasoning)

¼ teaspoon garlic powder

¼ teaspoon salt

Freshly ground black pepper, to taste

1. Preheat the oven to 425°F (220°C, or gas mark 7) convection (if available). Line a baking sheet with parchment paper.
2. Place the Brussels sprouts on the prepared baking sheet and drizzle with the olive oil. Toss using tongs. Sprinkle with the herb seasoning, garlic powder, salt, and pepper.
3. Roast until some of the leaves and bottoms become browned and crispy, about 10 minutes. Remove from the oven and stir. Roast some more until tender and most of the sprouts' outer leaves are browned and crispy.

RECIPE NOTE

You can buy Brussels sprouts while they are still on the stalk, which you can find at farmers' markets and some higher-end grocery stores. At the stores, look for nice and green, plump (not browned) outer leaves.

PER SERVING: 98 CALORIES | 8 G CARBOHYDRATE (3 G FIBER | 0 G ADDED SUGARS | 5 G NET CARBS) | 3 G PROTEIN | 7 G FAT | 167 MG SODIUM

Wispy Pan-Fried Zucchini

You can enroll in a cooking class at farm/restaurant Fattoria Terranova, just outside of Sorrento, Italy, a substantial town with breathtaking views of the Amalfi Coast. The simplicity of their garden-fresh zucchini, thinly sliced and lightly fried in olive oil, inspired this recipe.

TOTAL PREP AND COOK TIME: 20 minutes **YIELD:** 4 servings, ½ cup (125 g) each

Extra-virgin olive oil, for frying

4 smallish zucchini, thinly sliced

¼ teaspoon salt

1 tablespoon (15 ml) white wine vinegar

¼ cup (7 g) coarsely chopped fresh mint

1. Line a large plate or platter with a few layers of paper towel.
2. Pour the olive oil into a skillet until it is about ¼ inch (6 mm) deep. Heat the oil over medium heat for a few minutes. Do not let it get to the smoke point. When the oil begins to shimmer, you can test it by adding a zucchini slice; it should immediately start bubbling around the edges. When the oil is the right temperature, add the zucchini to the pan. You may need to cook it in batches. Cook until it becomes golden on one side, then turn, about 5 minutes total. Lift the zucchini using a spider skimmer, fish spatula, or slotted spoon. Sprinkle with the salt, vinegar, and mint.

PER SERVING: 83 CALORIES | 4 G CARBOHYDRATE (1 G FIBER | 0 G ADDED SUGARS | 3 G NET CARBS) | 2 G PROTEIN | 7 G FAT | 156 MG SODIUM

Baked Eggplant and Peppers with Garlic

You'll love the mellow, earthiness of eggplant. It's like a sponge, soaking up whatever flavors you pair with it.

TOTAL PREP AND COOK TIME: 45 minutes | **YIELD:** 6 servings, ½ cup (133 g) each

1 medium eggplant, cut into bite-size cubes

1 medium red or green bell pepper, cut into bite-size pieces

2 cloves garlic, minced

2 tablespoons (30 ml) extra-virgin olive oil, plus more for drizzling

¼ teaspoon salt

Pinch of crushed red pepper flakes

Freshly ground black pepper, to taste

1. Preheat the oven to 350°F (180°C, or gas mark 4).
2. Combine all of the ingredients in a 9 × 13-inch (23 × 33 cm) baking dish.
3. Bake until the vegetables become tender, about 30 minutes.
4. Drizzle with more oil for a richer taste.

PER SERVING: 60 CALORIES | 5 G CARBOHYDRATE (2 G FIBER | 0 G ADDED SUGARS | 3 G NET CARBS) | 1 G PROTEIN | 5 G FAT | 99 MG SODIUM

Sautéed Rainbow Swiss Chard

Rainbow Swiss chard is a nice way to mix things up in the greens department. It's a little heartier than other greens like spinach, but still tender.

TOTAL PREP AND COOK TIME: 20 minutes **YIELD:** 4 servings, ½ cup (87 g) each

1 bunch (11 ounces [310 g]) Swiss chard

1 tablespoon (15 ml) extra-virgin olive oil

1 clove garlic, minced

Pinch of crushed red pepper flakes

1 teaspoon red wine vinegar

⅛ teaspoon salt

Freshly ground black pepper, to taste

1. First, prep the chard: Using a sharp knife (you can use an agile boning knife for this), cut the ribs (the firm, center vein) away from the leaves, reserving the stems. Cut off the bottom ¼ inch (6 mm) of the ribs. Cut the ribs into manageable 4-inch (10 cm) or so pieces. Cut each piece lengthwise into equal-size strips. Then dice. Tear the leaves into smaller pieces.

2. Heat a large sauté pan over medium heat. Add the oil. When the oil is shimmering, add the diced ribs, garlic, and red pepper flakes. Cook until tender, about 5 minutes. Add the leaves and cook until wilted and tender, about 5 minutes, reducing the heat as needed. Add the red wine vinegar, salt, and pepper and stir to combine.

RECIPE NOTE

If you happen to sear meat with this meal, cook the chard in the same pan with the browned bits in the bottom of the pan for added flavor.

PER SERVING: 46 CALORIES | 3 G CARBOHYDRATE (1 G FIBER | 0 G ADDED SUGARS | 2 G NET CARBS) | 1 G PROTEIN | 4 G FAT | 239 MG SODIUM

Roasted Broccoli with Sumac

While you may love steamed, boiled, or microwaved broccoli, roasting broccoli takes it to a whole other level. With crispy, browned florets and stems, this broccoli is gobbled up straight from the baking sheet before it can even be served on the plate. Even the stems are so good in this, so you won't have any food waste. Keep the broccoli nice and long. Splitting them lengthwise once or twice helps cut down on cooking time. The key to the crispiness is to crank your oven high enough, and on the convection setting, if you have it.

TOTAL PREP AND COOK TIME: 20 minutes **YIELD:** 4 servings

1 pound (455 g) broccoli (1 medium head), cut into stalks, then split

2 tablespoons (30 ml) extra-virgin olive oil

¼ teaspoon garlic powder

¼ teaspoon salt

Freshly ground black pepper, to taste

1 teaspoon ground sumac (see Recipe Note)

1. Preheat the oven to 425°F (220°C, or gas mark 7) convection (if available). Line a baking sheet with parchment paper.
2. Place the broccoli on the prepared baking sheet and drizzle with the olive oil. Toss using tongs. Sprinkle with the garlic powder, salt, and pepper. Roast for 15 minutes, until sizzling and browned on the bottom. Remove from the oven and sprinkle with the sumac.

RECIPE NOTE

If you don't have or can't find sumac, add lemon zest before cooking, and spritz on lemon juice after cooking. Or a lemon pepper seasoning can also do the trick.

PER SERVING: 99 CALORIES | 7 G CARBOHYDRATE (3 G FIBER | 0 G ADDED SUGARS | 4 G NET CARBS) | 3 G PROTEIN | 7 G FAT | 183 MG SODIUM

3-Ingredient Avocado Truffles with Pistachios

You'll love the simplicity and ease of making these creamy, savory bites. Using avocados that are just ripe is key in this recipe, which means the fruit yields to gentle pressure, but is not soft. The skin should be speckly and blackish, with some green spots left.

TOTAL PREP AND COOK TIME: 20 minutes **YIELD:** 12 servings, 1 ball each

3 tablespoons (27 g) shelled pistachios, finely chopped

1 teaspoon za'atar seasoning blend (see Recipe Note)

1 large just-ripe avocado

1. Combine the pistachios and za'atar in a wide, shallow container.

2. Using a ½-teaspoon measuring spoon that is half sphere–shaped, scoop the avocado to make an avocado ball, like you are scooping the perfect ball of ice cream. Fill any small gaps with avocado and smooth with a butter knife as needed. Roll the avocado ball gently in the pistachios to coat evenly. Repeat the process for the 11 other truffles. It is best to enjoy these on the same day that you make them.

SUGGESTIONS AND VARIATIONS

You can play around with the types of seasonings and nuts, like toasted walnuts or almonds.

RECIPE NOTE

Za'atar is a Middle Eastern spice blend that has been around for ages, yet has been trending recently. Made of mostly sesame seeds, thyme, sumac, and salt, it offers an aromatic and herbal taste. You can find it in well-stocked grocery stores or you can make your own. You can use up the rest of the bottle by sprinkling on roasted vegetables, chicken, and a plain yogurt dip drizzled with olive oil.

PER SERVING: 30 CALORIES | 1 G CARBOHYDRATE (1 G FIBER | 0 G ADDED SUGARS | 0 G NET CARBS) | 1 G PROTEIN | 3 G FAT | 4 MG SODIUM

Mediterranean Tradition

You don't have to travel to North Africa to enjoy grilled sweet potatoes! To make your own, simply halve them, brush them with olive oil, and place them over a moderately heated grill, turning occasionally, until soft. Alternately, you can cut them into 1-inch (2.5 cm) cubes, brush them with olive oil and salt, wrap them in foil, and place them over a grill. Cook, turning halfway through, for 10 minutes on each side, or until soft.

North African Spice-Dusted Sweet Potatoes

Although potatoes were actually introduced into the Mediterranean after the Spaniards brought them back from the New World, they gained popularity in a short time. Along the Mediterranean shores of many North African countries, sweet potatoes are grilled over coals and sold on the street. Couples usually stop by and pick them up during their romantic evening strolls. Therefore, the Arabic term, *Qul Batatas,* or "Eating Potatoes," is often synonymous with being in love.

TOTAL PREP AND COOK TIME: 1 hour, 10 minutes **YIELD:** 4 servings

2 sweet potatoes, about ½ pound (225 g) each, scrubbed

2 tablespoons (30 ml) extra-virgin olive oil

1 teaspoon unrefined sea salt or salt

1 tablespoon (6 g) freshly ground black pepper

1 teaspoon pure cinnamon

1. Preheat the oven to 400°F (200°C). Prick the sweet potatoes with a fork and place in the middle of the oven. Bake for about 1 hour, or until soft when pressed.

2. Halve the sweet potatoes by splitting lengthwise and make crisscross cuts in the flesh. Drizzle the olive oil evenly over the flesh of the four halves. Sprinkle the salt, pepper, and cinnamon over each one. Serve hot.

NOTE: *Cinnamon, native to Asia and introduced to Africa by European traders, has been enjoyed in the Mediterranean since antiquity. It has been found to regulate blood sugar levels of people with type 2 diabetes. (The study used pure cinnamon, not the common American variety that contains cassia.) Pure cinnamon—sometimes called true cinnamon, Ceylon cinnamon, or Sri Lankan cinnamon—is becoming more readily available in the United States and has a milder, sweeter, flavor. The consumption of sweet potatoes is believed to help balance the glycemic index of diabetics. When paired together, both their taste and nutritional benefits are powerful!*

PER SERVING: 160 CALORIES | 24 G CARBOHYDRATE (4 G FIBER | 0 G ADDED SUGARS | 20 G NET CARBS) | 2 G PROTEIN | 7 G FAT | 650 MG SODIUM

Potatoes with Kale, Garlic, Olive Oil, and Chile Pepper

This delicious side dish is a nutritional powerhouse! Potatoes contain antioxidants and phytochemicals that strengthen the immune system, lower inflammation, and prevent tumor growth. According to webmd.com, "One cup of chopped kale contains 33 calories and 9% of the daily value of calcium, 206% of vitamin A, 134% of vitamin C, and a whopping 684% of vitamin K."

TOTAL PREP AND COOK TIME: 45 minutes **YIELD:** 4 servings

4 medium Yukon Gold potatoes, chopped into bite-size pieces

4 tablespoons (60 ml) extra-virgin olive oil, divided

4 cloves garlic, finely chopped

Crushed red chile pepper

Unrefined sea salt or salt

Freshly ground black pepper, to taste

½ pound (225 g) fresh kale, rinsed with stems and tough ribs discarded, then roughly chopped

1. Preheat the oven to 450°F (230°C).
2. Place the potatoes on a baking sheet and combine them with 2 tablespoons (30 ml) of oil, garlic, crushed red chile pepper, salt, and black pepper, and bake for 15 to 20 minutes, until golden and soft.
3. In a large bowl, toss the kale with the remaining 2 tablespoons (30 ml) of oil along with salt and pepper to taste. When the potatoes have roasted, remove from the oven and scatter the kale on top of them. Return to the oven and roast for another 10 minutes, or until the kale is crisp. Serve hot.

Mediterranean Tradition

Kale is one of the few vegetables that grows well in cooler temperatures. It can be sautéed, added into soups and pasta dishes, eaten raw in salad, or baked. Choose kale that has strong, deeply colored leaves with thick stems. Fresh kale can be wrapped in paper towels and stored, unwashed, in airtight zippered plastic bags for up to five days in the refrigerator.

PER SERVING: 310 CALORIES | 41 G CARBOHYDRATE (7 G FIBER | 0 G ADDED SUGARS | 34 G NET CARBS) | 6 G PROTEIN | 15 G FAT | 45 MG SODIUM

Mediterranean Tradition

It's said that there are 60 million olive trees in Puglia—one for every Italian. A drizzle of great Puglia olive oil brings this humble dish to life. Do as the Italians do: Use a basic first cold-pressed, extra-virgin olive oil for cooking. Then, buy the best-quality unfiltered olive oil to drizzle on top of dishes such as this one.

Fava Beans with Chicory

This recipe is from *The Al Tiramisu Restaurant Cookbook* by Luigi Diotaiuti, who says, "Natives of Puglia in southern Italy proudly associate this dish with their culinary patrimony. But it's also popular in parts of my region, which shares a border with Puglia." Recipes for this dish can vary—almost from one household to another. Fava beans, one of the world's oldest agricultural crops, have long been a staple of southern Italian cooking. But thanks to Queen Margherita, wife of King Umberto of the Kingdom of Italy in the late 1800s, this dish and other 'street food' were introduced to Italian nobility and eventually the rest of the world. Serve this dish alone or as part of a mixed appetizer platter. Note that the fava beans must be soaked overnight.

TOTAL PREP AND COOK TIME: 45 minutes **YIELD:** 4 servings

11 ounces (312 g) dried peeled fava beans, placed in a bowl, covered with boiling water (4 inches [10 cm] above top of beans), and left to soak overnight

½ small onion

4 ounces (115 g) potatoes, diced

1 teaspoon unrefined sea salt or salt

7 ounces (198 g) chicory or dandelion greens, cleaned

⅓ cup (80 ml) good-quality olive oil, preferably from Puglia, divided

2 cloves garlic, thinly sliced

1. Drain the soaked fava beans and place them in a medium saucepan.
2. Add the onion, potatoes, and salt. Cover with water and bring to a boil over high heat. Reduce heat to medium-low, cover, and cook until the beans are tender, about 25 minutes. This could take longer depending on the size of the beans.
3. In a medium saucepan, cook the chicory or dandelion greens in enough salted boiling water to cover for 2 minutes. Drain and reserve the cooking liquid.
4. Transfer the beans and vegetables to a food processor or food mill. Purée until smooth, adding a tablespoon (15 ml) of the olive oil and additional salt, if needed. Add a few tablespoons of the reserved cooking water, if needed. Heat a tablespoon (15 ml) of olive oil in a medium skillet over medium heat. Add the garlic and cook until it turns golden, about 1 minute. Add the chicory or dandelion greens. Stir well and cook for a couple minutes, to absorb flavors. Season with salt to taste.
5. To serve, spread the fava purée in the bottom of a terra-cotta bowl. Mound the chicory in the center. Drizzle the remaining olive oil on top and serve.

PER SERVING: 460 CALORIES | 54 G CARBOHYDRATE (22 G FIBER | 0 G ADDED SUGARS | 32 G NET CARBS) | 22 G PROTEIN | 19 G FAT | 620 MG SODIUM

Chickpea Fritters

This recipe is essentially a simplified version of falafel made with canned chickpeas, but ready in just 20 minutes with a handful of pantry ingredients you probably have on hand. Serve with plain Greek yogurt or the Cucumber Yogurt Salad on page 72.

TOTAL PREP AND COOK TIME: 20 minutes | **YIELD:** 3 patties each

1 clove garlic, peeled

1 can (15-ounce [425 g]) chickpeas, rinsed and drained

1 stalk celery, cut into chunks

3 tablespoons (45 ml) extra-virgin olive oil, divided

1 lemon, zest finely grated, plus 1 tablespoon (15 ml) juice

½ teaspoon ground cumin

¼ teaspoon salt

Freshly ground black pepper, to taste

Fresh chopped chives, mint, or Italian flat-leaf parsley, optional, for garnish

1. Mince the garlic in a food processor. Add the chickpeas, celery, 1 tablespoon (15 ml) of the oil, lemon zest and juice, cumin, salt, and pepper. Pulse until it forms a chunky shapeable mixture, but is not smooth. Scoop into 9 balls, about 2 tablespoons (30 g) each. Squish into thick patties.
2. Heat a large sauté pan over medium heat. Add 1 tablespoon (15 ml) oil. When the oil is shimmering, add the patties and cook until golden, about 4 minutes. Carefully turn (the patties are on the fragile side) with a fish spatula or small flexible turner; you may need to add the remaining 1 tablespoon (15 ml) oil. Brown on the other side, another 3 to 4 minutes. Transfer to a plate lined with paper towels. Serve with a sprinkle of herbs.

PER SERVING: 205 CALORIES | 14 G CARBOHYDRATE (4 G FIBER | 0 G ADDED SUGARS | 10 G NET CARBS) | 5 G PROTEIN | 15 G FAT | 461 MG SODIUM

Roasted Spaghetti Squash and Tomatoes

Part "pasta," part vegetable, 100 percent delicious. Roasted spaghetti squash makes for a delicious side dish or base for chicken, Bolognese sauce, and more.

TOTAL PREP AND COOK TIME: 1 hour

YIELD: 4 servings, 1 cup (155 g) each

1 small spaghetti squash (1½ to 2 pounds [680 to 910 g])

2 tablespoons (30 ml) extra-virgin olive oil, divided

¼ teaspoon salt, divided, plus more to taste

Freshly ground black pepper, to taste

1 cup (150 g) cherry tomatoes, halved

¼ teaspoon dried thyme

¼ cup (10 g) fresh basil leaves, with the larger ones hand-torn

1. Preheat the oven to 375°F (190°C, or gas mark 4). Line a baking sheet with a silicone baking mat or parchment paper.
2. Slice off the top and bottom ¼ inch (6 mm) of the squash. Cut the squash in half lengthwise and scoop out the seeds. Drizzle with 1 tablespoon (15 ml) of the oil and season with ⅛ teaspoon of the salt and some pepper. Place the squash on one side of the prepared baking sheet, cut-side down.
3. On a piece of foil, about 10 × 10 inches (25 × 25 cm), spread the tomatoes in a single layer and top with 2 teaspoons (10 ml) of the oil, the thyme, the remaining ⅛ teaspoon salt, and some pepper. Fold all sides of the foil straight up to create an edge, keeping the juices and oil inside as it bakes. Move the foil boat to the pan.
4. Bake the squash and tomatoes until tender and softened, about 30 minutes. Carefully remove the foil boat from the pan. Continue to bake the squash until it is sizzling around the edges and a fork pierces very easily through the skin, about 10 minutes more.
5. Carefully turn the squash over to release the steam. When it is cool enough to handle, shred the squash with a fork to create strands. When the fork is no longer pulling up strands, you can use a spoon to scrape the remaining squash from the skin.

6. To serve, place the squash in a shallow bowl or platter. Sprinkle the tomatoes on top, drizzle with the remaining 1 teaspoon (5 ml) oil, fresh basil leaves, and salt and pepper to taste.

PER SERVING: 130 CALORIES | 16 G CARBOHYDRATE (4 G FIBER | 0 G ADDED SUGARS | 12 G NET CARBS) | 2 G PROTEIN | 8 G FAT | 182 MG SODIUM

Roasted Cauliflower with Cashews and Turmeric

It is surprising how satisfying and filling this cauliflower can be!

TOTAL PREP AND COOK TIME: 30 minutes **YIELD:** 4 servings, 1 cup (270 g) each

- 1 small head cauliflower, cut into bite-size florets (about 6 cups, or 600 g)
- 1 teaspoon ground turmeric
- ½ teaspoon garlic powder
- ½ teaspoon ground cumin
- ¼ teaspoon salt
- Freshly ground black pepper, to taste
- 2 tablespoons (30 ml) extra-virgin olive oil
- ¼ cup (32 g) roasted cashews, chopped through twice (or use slivered or sliced almonds)

1. Preheat the oven to 425°F (220°C, or gas mark 7) convection (if available). Line a baking sheet with parchment paper or a silicone baking mat.
2. Place the cauliflower on the prepared baking sheet. In a small bowl, combine the turmeric, garlic powder, cumin, salt, and pepper. Drizzle the cauliflower with the oil. Sprinkle with the seasonings. Sprinkle on the cashews. Roast until the cauliflower is fork-tender, about 15 minutes.

PER SERVING: 150 CALORIES | 11 G CARBOHYDRATE (3 G FIBER | 0 G ADDED SUGARS | 8 G NET CARBS) | 4 G PROTEIN | 11 G FAT | 193 MG SODIUM

Baked Stuffed Artichokes

While canned or jarred artichokes are super-quick toppers, fresh artichokes provide an elevated taste and textural experience. It's really just the artichoke heart that is worth eating—which is at the core of this plant and also runs down the center of the stem.

There are two ways to get to the creamy core. One way is a bit laborious, accomplished by cutting away all of the leaves and peeling the stem.

The method used in this recipe is easier. You just stuff the goodies into the center and bake the entire artichoke, and eat it by placing a leaf between your teeth, pulling off the creamy center. You can use bread crumbs, but in this version they are swapped out with almond flour.

TOTAL PREP AND COOK TIME: 45 minutes **YIELD:** 4 servings, ¼ artichoke each

1 large artichoke

2 tablespoons (12 g) unpacked almond flour

2 tablespoons (10 g) grated Parmesan cheese

2 tablespoons (30 ml) lemon juice, divided

1 clove garlic, minced

¼ teaspoon salt

Freshly ground black pepper, to taste

2 tablespoons (30 ml) extra-virgin olive oil

1. Preheat the oven to 350°F (180°C, or gas mark 4).
2. Cut the very tips of the artichoke leaves with kitchen shears about ½ inch (12 mm) from the top.
3. Trim a slice off from the stem. Quarter the artichoke lengthwise. Scoop out the "fur" with a spoon.
4. In a bowl, combine the almond flour, Parmesan, 1 tablespoon (15 ml) of the lemon juice, garlic, salt, and pepper. Place the artichoke in a baking dish, cut-side up. Stuff the filling into the scooped-out core and drizzle with olive oil. Cover and bake until the artichoke is fork-tender in the middle, about 20 minutes. Drizzle with the remaining 1 tablespoon (15 ml) lemon juice.
5. To serve, remove the leaves of the artichoke, and pull a leaf through your teeth. Also don't miss out on the creamy center core.

PER SERVING: 112 CALORIES | 6 G CARBOHYDRATE (2 G FIBER | 0 G ADDED SUGARS | 4 G NET CARBS) | 2 G PROTEIN | 9 G FAT | 211 MG SODIUM

Spaghetti with Garlic, Oil, and Chile Pepper

Many Italian, first-course pasta dishes are tossed with fresh vegetables and herbs instead of ladled with a heavy sauce. This spaghetti dish pairs beautifully with heavier, tomato-sauce-laden second courses, such as eggplant or chicken parmigiana, or stewed fish, chicken, or meat dishes. This mixture also tastes great drizzled over grilled, steamed, or blanched vegetables.

TOTAL PREP AND COOK TIME: 25 minutes **YIELD:** 8 servings (as a first course)

½ teaspoon kosher or sea salt

1 pound (455 g) spaghetti or gluten-free alternative

¼ cup (60 ml) extra-virgin olive oil, plus extra for drizzling

8 cloves garlic, minced

¼ teaspoon crushed red chili flakes

1 bunch fresh, flat-leaf parsley, finely chopped

⅛ teaspoon freshly ground black pepper

¼ cup (30 g) freshly grated Pecorino cheese

1. Bring a large pot of water to a boil over high heat. Add the salt. Add the pasta and toss.
2. Reduce heat to medium-low, and cook, uncovered, until very al dente (see package directions for various pastas), and drain well.
3. While the pasta is cooking, heat the olive oil in a large, wide skillet over medium heat. Add the garlic and chili flakes, and cook just until they release their aroma, 30 to 60 seconds. Add the pasta and parsley to the skillet, and toss to coat. Drizzle with additional olive oil, if desired. Add black pepper to taste and serve immediately with Pecorino cheese.

Mediterranean Tradition

Quick, comforting pasta dishes such as this one are to Italians what pub food is to the Americans and the British. These are the dishes that one eats on occasion to satisfy a craving or to fill one's stomach after a night out with friends. While the carbohydrate-heavy dish isn't the most healthful in this book, it is extremely satisfying, and much more nutritious than fast food. If you don't suffer from gluten sensitivity, seek out pasta made from durum wheat, which offers a higher amount of protein and other nutrients.

PER SERVING: 290 CALORIES | 45 G CARBOHYDRATE (3 G FIBER | 0 G ADDED SUGARS | 42 G NET CARBS) | 8 G PROTEIN | 9 G FAT | 170 MG SODIUM

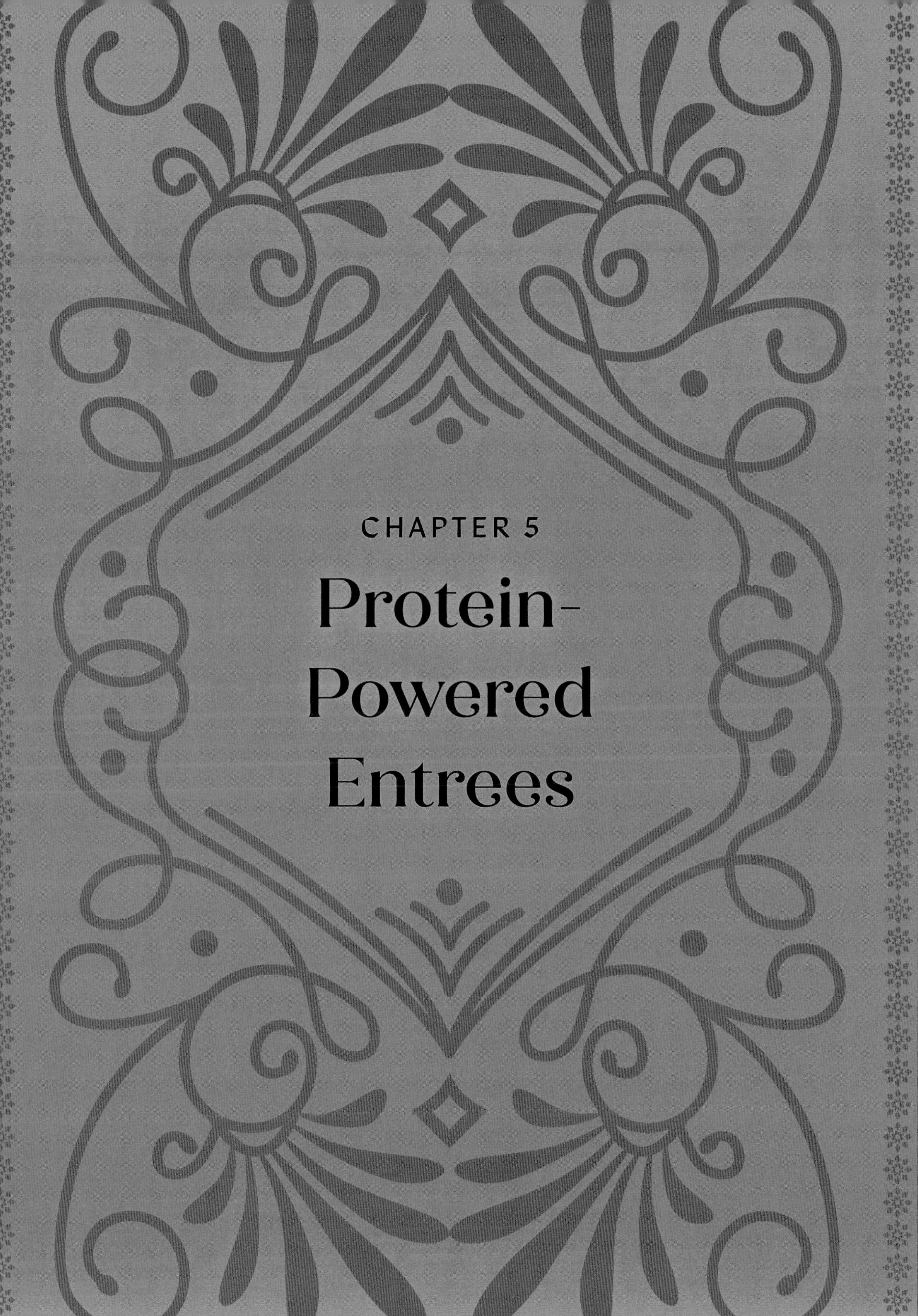

CHAPTER 5

Protein-Powered Entrees

Italian Halibut with Grapes and Olive Oil

Creative chefs in Italian coastal regions sometimes swap grapes for the tomatoes in a dish called *pesce in acqua pazza,* or "fish in crazy water." It's called crazy water because crushed red chilies give the cooking water a kick. Typically, freshly caught sea bream is used, although you can substitute halibut for its easy access and high omega-3 content in this recipe. It's said that this dish can transport someone from a rainy day in London to the sunny Italian Riviera.

TOTAL PREP AND COOK TIME: 25 minutes | **YIELD:** 4 servings

¼ cup (60 ml) extra-virgin olive oil

4 boneless halibut fillets (4 ounces, or 115 g, each)

4 cloves garlic, roughly chopped

1 small red chile pepper, finely chopped

2 cups (300 g) seedless green grapes

A handful of fresh basil leaves, roughly torn

½ teaspoon sea salt

Freshly ground black pepper, to taste

1. Heat the olive oil in a large, heavy-bottomed skillet over medium-high heat. Add the halibut, followed by the garlic, chile pepper, grapes, basil, and salt and pepper. Pour in 1¾ cups (410 ml) of water, turn the heat down to medium-low, cover, and cook the fish until opaque, or for 7 minutes on each side.

2. Remove the fish from the pan and place on a large serving dish. Raise the heat, and cook the sauce for 30 seconds to concentrate the flavors slightly. Taste and adjust the salt and pepper. Pour the sauce over the fish.

Mediterranean Tradition

Phytonutrients in grapes are believed to contribute to longevity. Try incorporating them into recipes for a surprising fresh, sweet-and-sour flavor.

PER SERVING: 290 CALORIES | 15 G CARBOHYDRATE (1 G FIBER | 0 G ADDED SUGARS | 15 G NET CARBS) | 22 G PROTEIN | 16 G FAT | 370 MG SODIUM

Broiled Flounder with Lemon, Parsley, and Garlic

Flounder is a whitefish similar to halibut in taste and texture, but in smaller fillets. The word *flounder* is a general term for flatfish species such as fluke, dab, and lemon sole. This is a great standby recipe in a rotation, since it is so easy to make with any type of whitefish and staple ingredients you always have on hand. While you may not see flounder everywhere in fresh fish cases, you may find it in the freezer section in common grocery stores. You may also substitute with tilapia, but since tilapia fillets can be quite large, increase the cooking time as needed.

TOTAL PREP AND COOK TIME: 25 minutes **YIELD:** 4 servings

Cooking oil spray

1 pound (455 g) flounder fillets (about 4 fillets), patted dry

1 tablespoon (15 ml) extra-virgin olive oil, plus more for drizzling

1 lemon, zest finely grated, then fruit cut into wedges

1 clove garlic, sliced

¼ teaspoon salt

Freshly ground black pepper, to taste

¼ cup (15 g) coarsely chopped Italian flat-leaf parsley

1 teaspoon capers, chopped (optional)

1. Move an oven rack to 6 inches (15 cm) below the broiler. Preheat the oven to low broil. Line a baking sheet with foil for easier cleanup. Coat the foil with oil spray.
2. Place the fish on the prepared baking sheet. In a small bowl, combine the oil, lemon zest, garlic, salt, and pepper and spread on top of the fish. Broil until the edges are sizzling and the centers are opaque white, about 10 minutes, though cooking time will vary depending on the thickness of the fillets.
3. Sprinkle with the parsley and capers, if using and serve with the lemon wedges. Drizzle with additional oil, if desired.

Make It for the Whole Family

On nights you cook whitefish prepared with a variety of ingredients, you can reserve a fillet for pickier eaters. Cut up the fillet into finger-size pieces and simply season them with salt. Cook the fish on the same pan as the other fish, but perhaps in a little foil "boat" to keep it away from other flavors.

PER SERVING: 151 CALORIES | 1 G CARBOHYDRATE (0 G FIBER | 0 G ADDED SUGARS | 1 G NET CARBS) | 1 G PROTEIN | 9 G FAT | 456 MG SODIUM

Moroccan-Style Grilled Tuna

When we think of Moroccan cuisine, lamb, couscous, and tajines usually come to mind. Bordering both the Mediterranean Sea and Atlantic Ocean, however, Morocco offers a wonderful array of flavors from the sea. This recipe features chermoula sauce, a Moroccan classic that tastes great on both chicken and fish. If you prefer to make this dish in the oven, instead of grilling it, simply place the fish in a greased baking dish, top with chermoula, cover with aluminum foil, and bake in a 425°F (220°C) oven for 20 to 25 minutes, or until cooked through.

TOTAL PREP AND COOK TIME: 1 hour, 20 minutes **YIELD:** 4 servings

2 tablespoons (5 g) finely chopped cilantro

2 tablespoons (5 g) finely chopped parsley

6 cloves garlic, minced

½ teaspoon unrefined sea salt or salt

½ teaspoon paprika

1 lemon, juiced and zested

3 tablespoons (45 ml) extra-virgin olive oil

4 tuna steaks (4 ounces, or 115 g, each)

1. In a medium bowl, mix the cilantro, parsley, garlic, salt, paprika, and lemon juice and zest together. Whisk in the olive oil.
2. Place the fish in a glass baking dish and pour half of the chermoula sauce over the top. Cover with plastic wrap and allow to marinate for 1 hour.
3. Preheat the grill to medium-high heat.
4. Grill the fish, turning once, until firm, 6 to 8 minutes. Transfer to a platter, spread with the remaining chermoula sauce, and let stand for 5 minutes to absorb the flavors.

Mediterranean Tradition

Marinating seafood, meat, and chicken before grilling it not only flavors it, but also reduces the harmful cancer-causing substances that can result from cooking over an open flame.

PER SERVING: 220 CALORIES | 3 G CARBOHYDRATE (0 G FIBER | 0 G ADDED SUGARS | 2 G NET CARBS) | 28 G PROTEIN | 11 G FAT | 350 MG SODIUM

Sizzling Rosemary Shrimp over Polenta

Think of this recipe as the Mediterranean cousin of shrimp and grits. The savory, flash-sautéed shrimp taste great on their own as a tapa or tossed into spaghetti or linguine with olive oil and lemon zest. Serving them over polenta, a traditional staple in Italy since the sixteenth century, rounds out the meal.

TOTAL PREP AND COOK TIME: 15 minutes | **YIELD:** 6 servings

¼ cup (60 ml) extra-virgin olive oil

2 cloves garlic, minced

1½ pounds (680 g) prawns or jumbo shrimp, peeled and deveined

2 teaspoons freshly chopped rosemary

Dash of crushed red chili flakes

½ teaspoon kosher salt

¼ teaspoon freshly ground black pepper

3 cups cooked polenta

1. Heat the olive oil in a large skillet over medium-high heat. Add the garlic and stir. Add the prawns or shrimp, rosemary, chili flakes, salt, and pepper.
2. Cook, uncovered, for about 2 minutes per side, or until the prawns or shrimp turn pink. Spoon the polenta onto a serving platter evenly, and flatten with the back of a spoon. Place the prawns or shrimp on top and serve immediately.

Mediterranean Tradition

Known for a wide variety of health benefits, fresh and dried rosemary along with rosemary oil, tonics, and tea is used daily in the Mediterranean. It is believed that its aroma boosts brainpower. It also possesses antiviral properties and is known to relieve pain and ease menstrual disorders, kidney stones, and digestion, as well as increase the appetite and help with gallbladder, liver, and heart problems. Rosemary oil is massaged into the scalp for stronger, darker hair and to alleviate dandruff and skin problems.

PER SERVING: 280 CALORIES | 19 G CARBOHYDRATE (1 G FIBER | 0 G ADDED SUGARS | 18 G NET CARBS) | 24 G PROTEIN | 13 G FAT | 440 MG SODIUM

Citrus-Marinated Scallops

This delicious and impressive dish can be cooked in minutes and served as an appetizer or main course. These scallops also taste great when tossed into a salad or pasta, rice, and other grain-based dishes. In the United States, scallops are sometimes soaked in the preservative trisodium phosphate (TSP), which makes them weigh more, and consequently cost more. TSP also makes scallops exude moisture as they cook, thereby causing them to steam rather than sear properly. Look for scallops labeled dry, that is, not soaked in TSP.

TOTAL PREP AND COOK TIME: 1 hour, 15 minutes **YIELD:** 4 servings

Juice and zest of 2 lemons

¼ cup (60 ml) extra-virgin olive oil

Unrefined sea salt or salt, to taste

Freshly ground black pepper, to taste

1 clove garlic, minced

1½ pounds (680 g) dry scallops, side muscle removed

1. In a large shallow bowl or baking dish, combine the lemon juice and zest, olive oil, salt, pepper, and garlic. Mix well to combine. Add the scallops to the marinade; cover and refrigerate 1 hour.
2. Heat a large skillet over medium-high heat. Drain the scallops and place them in skillet. Cook 4 to 5 minutes per side, until cooked through.

Mediterranean Tradition

All throughout the region, scallops are increasingly being enjoyed raw in beautiful carpaccios. To make a carpaccio, simply place the scallops on a baking sheet lined with waxed paper. Cover with plastic wrap and place in the freezer for at least 1 hour. When the scallops are almost hard, remove them from the freezer, and with a sharp filleting knife, carefully cut the scallops widthwise into paper-thin slices. Place them on a platter. Drizzle with a vinaigrette and serve with greens. Note that consuming raw or undercooked seafood and shellfish may increase your risk of food-borne illness.

PER SERVING: 140 CALORIES | 3 G CARBOHYDRATE (0 G FIBER | 0 G ADDED SUGARS | 3 G NET CARBS) | 3 G PROTEIN | 14 G FAT | 90 MG SODIUM

Trout Cooked in Parchment

Moist and flavorful, this easy-to-clean cooking method is popular all over Italy. Trout is one of the fish with some of the highest amounts of omega-3s.

TOTAL PREP AND COOK TIME: 25 minutes **YIELD:** 4 servings

3 cloves garlic, finely chopped

8 fresh sage leaves, finely chopped

½ cup (30 g) finely chopped fresh parsley

Zest and juice of 1 lemon, plus an additional 1 lemon cut into wedges for serving

⅓ cup (80 ml) extra-virgin olive oil

1 teaspoon unrefined sea salt or salt

Freshly ground pepper, to taste

4 trout fillets (4 ounces, or 115 g, each)

1. Preheat the oven to 425°F (220°C). Combine the garlic, sage, parsley, lemon zest and juice, olive oil, salt, and pepper in a small bowl. Cut four pieces of parchment paper—each more than double the size of the trout.

2. Place 1 trout on top of each piece of parchment and equally distribute one quarter of garlic-herb mixture on each fish. Brush any remaining garlic-herb mixture over the fish and fold the parchment over the fish. Fold and crimp the edges to seal tightly and place in a baking dish.

3. Bake about 10 minutes, until the fish is cooked through. Remove from the oven, and serve with lemon wedges, allowing guests to open their own individual packages at the table.

Mediterranean Tradition

Thinly sliced vegetables such as fennel, eggplant, tomatoes, and zucchini could be baked alongside the fish in the parchment.

PER SERVING: 340 CALORIES | 3 G CARBOHYDRATE (0 G FIBER | 0 G ADDED SUGARS | 2 G NET CARBS) | 24 G PROTEIN | 26 G FAT | 650 MG SODIUM

Citrus-Marinated Salmon with Fennel Cream

Orange and salmon are a match made in heaven. The sweet citrus flavors combine with the rich, oily textures in the salmon for a healthful dish that seems too decadent to be good for you. Fennel and yogurt are two popular Mediterranean ingredients that are as virtuous as they are delicious.

TOTAL PREP AND COOK TIME: 1 hour, 45 minutes **YIELD:** 4 servings

2 tablespoons (30 ml) extra-virgin olive oil

2 oranges, 1 juiced and zested, 1 thinly sliced

½ teaspoon sea salt

Freshly ground black pepper, to taste

4 salmon fillets (4 ounces, or 115 g, each), skin on

1 fennel bulb, thinly sliced (reserve fronds)

½ sweet onion, thinly sliced

1 cup (230 g) plain Greek yogurt

1. In a small bowl, whisk the olive oil, orange juice, salt, and pepper together until emulsified.
2. Place the salmon fillets in a glass baking dish and pour the marinade over the top. Allow to marinate for 1 hour.
3. Preheat the oven to 400°F (200°C).
4. Scatter the fennel and onion around the sides of the salmon, and cover the baking dish with aluminum foil. Bake until the fish flakes easily with a fork and is opaque, 20 to 25 minutes.
5. While the fish is baking, combine the Greek yogurt with 2 tablespoons (6 g) fennel fronds, finely chopped, and the orange zest.
6. Remove the fish from the oven and place on a serving plate. Dollop each with about one-quarter of the yogurt mixture and garnish with the orange slices.

Mediterranean Tradition

Fennel, known to be a digestive aid, is often eaten raw in salads, braised, or roasted as in recipes such as this one. Its seeds are also used as a spice and boiled to make soothing after-dinner teas.

PER SERVING: 400 CALORIES | 18 G CARBOHYDRATE (4 G FIBER | 0 G ADDED SUGARS | 14 G NET CARBS) | 31 G PROTEIN | 24 G FAT | 420 MG SODIUM

Artichoke Omelette

You can use canned artichokes for convenience, but this omelette is particularly nice when you use fresh artichokes.

TOTAL PREP AND COOK TIME: 15 minutes **YIELD:** 4 servings

3 large eggs

2 tablespoons (5 g) finely chopped fresh parsley leaves

Salt and freshly ground black pepper, to taste

3 medium-size canned artichoke bottoms, finely chopped, or fresh artichokes, trimmed to their bottoms, cooked until tender, and finely chopped

1 garlic clove, finely chopped

1 tablespoon (5 g) freshly grated Parmigiano-Reggiano cheese

1 tablespoon (15 ml) extra-virgin olive oil

1. In a medium-size bowl, beat the eggs and parsley together and season with salt and pepper. Add the artichokes, garlic, and cheese and beat well.
2. In an 8-inch (20 cm) nonstick skillet or omelette pan, heat the olive oil over medium heat, then pour in the egg mixture and shake the pan while it sets, about 1 minute. Fold the omelette over with a metal spatula and cook another 30 seconds. Transfer to a plate and serve immediately.

PER SERVING: 100 CALORIES | 3 G CARBOHYDRATE (0 G FIBER | 0 G ADDED SUGARS | 2 G NET CARBS) | 6 G PROTEIN | 8 G FAT | 130 MG SODIUM

Poached Eggs in Garlicky Yogurt

This dish of poached eggs set in a garlicky and peppery sauce of thick yogurt called çilbir in Turkish seems so likely to be served for breakfast, but it is also served as a meze.

TOTAL PREP AND COOK TIME: 15 minutes **YIELD:** 4 servings

2 large garlic cloves, peeled

½ teaspoon salt, plus more for boiling water

2 cups (460 g) full-fat plain yogurt

3 tablespoons (42 g) unsalted butter

½ teaspoon Turkish red pepper or a mixture of 2 parts sweet paprika and 1 part cayenne pepper

4 large eggs

Crusty French or Italian bread

1. In a mortar, pound the garlic with the salt until mushy. In a medium-size bowl, beat the yogurt with a fork until smooth, then beat in the garlic paste.
2. In a butter warmer or small saucepan, melt the butter and stir in the red pepper.
3. Bring a few inches of water to a boil in a large saucepan, add some salt, and stir in one direction to start a gentle whirlpool. Break the eggs rapidly in succession into the swirling boiling water. Do this carefully and close to the water by spilling the egg out of its shell. Cook until the white is set but the yolk is runny, about 2 minutes. Remove the eggs with a slotted ladle, arrange them in shallow individual serving bowls, and spoon ½ cup of the yogurt over the whites of each egg. Drizzle the butter-and-pepper mixture over the eggs and serve immediately with fresh crusty bread.

PER SERVING: 230 CALORIES | 7 G CARBOHYDRATE (0 G FIBER | 0 G ADDED SUGARS | 7 G NET CARBS) | 11 G PROTEIN | 18 G FAT | 410 MG SODIUM

Baked Salmon with Parsley and Garlic Crust

Cook fresh salmon during peak salmon season, which is during the summer months. The addition of herbs and lemon accents the fish nicely, without overpowering it.

TOTAL PREP AND COOK TIME: 30 minutes **YIELD:** 4 servings

¼ cup (15 g) coarsely chopped parsley leaves

1 lemon, zest finely grated, then fruit cut into wedges

1 tablespoon (11 g) Dijon mustard

1 clove garlic, minced

1 tablespoon (15 ml) extra-virgin olive oil

1 pound (455 g) salmon fillet, whole or cut into 4 pieces

¼ teaspoon salt

Freshly ground black pepper, to taste

1. Preheat the oven to 350°F (180°C, or gas mark 3). Line a baking sheet with parchment paper or a silicone baking mat.
2. Combine the parsley, lemon zest, Dijon, garlic, and olive oil in a small bowl.
3. Place the salmon on the prepared baking sheet. Season the salmon all over with salt and pepper. Spoon the parsley mixture on top of the salmon. Bake until it's sizzling around the edges and medium in the center, before it becomes firm, about 20 minutes. The exact time will depend on the thickness of the salmon, and if you are baking individual portions of salmon, it will cook in about 15 to 20 minutes. Serve with the lemon wedges.

SUGGESTIONS AND VARIATIONS

If you keep an herb garden in the summer and have a range of varieties like chives, basil, and dill, feel free to mix those in with the parsley.

Make It for the Whole Family

Your kids might appreciate small nuggets of salmon, simply seasoned with just salt. These pieces will cook quicker, in about 10 minutes.

PER SERVING: 182 CALORIES | 1 G CARBOHYDRATE (0 G FIBER | 0 G ADDED SUGARS | 1 G NET CARBS) | 24 G PROTEIN | 9 G FAT | 322 MG SODIUM

Lemon Baked Cod with Pistachio Crust

This 30-minute recipe is light and satisfying, offering a nice crunch from the pistachios. This flavor profile would also work great on other seafoods available, like salmon, trout, and tilapia.

TOTAL PREP AND COOK TIME: 30 minutes **YIELD:** 4 servings

3 tablespoons (45 ml) extra-virgin olive oil

1 lemon, zest finely grated, then fruit cut into wedges

1 teaspoon Italian seasoning

¼ teaspoon salt

Freshly ground black pepper, to taste

1 pound (455 g) cod or pollock fillet, cut into 4 pieces

⅓ cup (37 g) roasted and salted shelled pistachios, finely chopped

1. Preheat the oven to 350°F (180°C, or gas mark 4). Line a baking sheet with parchment paper or a silicone baking mat.
2. In a small bowl, combine the olive oil, lemon zest, Italian seasoning, salt, and pepper.
3. Place the cod on the prepared baking sheet and spoon the seasoned oil on the fillet, rubbing it onto all sides. Dip the tops of the cod into the pistachios and press gently, forming a top crust, and place back on the pan.
4. Bake until the fish is sizzling around the edges and opaque and nearly firm in the middle, about 15 minutes. Serve with the lemon wedges.

SUGGESTIONS AND VARIATIONS

A great accompaniment with most seafood dishes is tartar sauce. You can make it quickly with just a handful of ingredients: mayonnaise, chopped dill pickles, lemon juice, Cajun seasoning, Dijon mustard, salt, and pepper. While it isn't required to make this dish, it is a nice addition if tartar sauce is a must for you.

Make It for the Whole Family

Your kids may be more inclined to try simple fish fingers. Cut up one of the fillets into strips and season with salt and pepper. You can bake them on the same pan, but they may cook a little faster than the other portions.

PER SERVING: 220 CALORIES | 3 G CARBOHYDRATE (1 G FIBER | 0 G ADDED SUGARS | 2 G NET CARBS) | 19 G PROTEIN | 15 G FAT | 489 MG SODIUM

Mediterranean Grilled Shrimp

While in Rovinj, Croatia, one of the most memorable meals is the simplest dish—fresh whole shrimp grilled in the shells. They are just bursting with juicy flavors of the sea. Since whole fresh shrimp isn't easy to come by, unless you live on the coast, this recipe was created using the kind you typically find with just the tails, but buy those with the shells on, which adds more shrimp flavor and keeps the shrimp moist. Marinate the shrimp first so the flavors seep beyond the shell.

TOTAL PREP AND COOK TIME: 45 minutes **YIELD:** 4 servings, about 3 shrimp each

1 pound (455 g) large in-shell shrimp, fresh or thawed (10/15 count size)

Fresh thyme sprigs

3 cloves garlic, smashed with wide side of knife

2 tablespoons (30 ml) extra-virgin olive oil

1 lemon, zest finely grated, then fruit cut into wedges

¼ teaspoon salt

Freshly ground black pepper, to taste

1. Blot the shrimp dry. Cut the shrimp the long way through the backs, about halfway through the meat. Place the shrimp in a shallow dish. Add the thyme and garlic, drizzle with the oil, and sprinkle on the lemon zest. Marinate for at least 30 minutes, up to a few hours.

2. When ready to cook the shrimp, preheat the grill to medium heat, about 350–400°F (180–200°C). Pull the shrimp from the fridge to allow them to temper. Sprinkle the shrimp with salt and pepper. Grill the shrimp until opaque nearly halfway through, a few minutes. Turn and cook through, a couple minutes more. Remove and spritz on lemon juice.

SUGGESTIONS AND VARIATIONS

To change up the flavors, try using an orange in place of the lemon, and other fresh herbs in place of thyme, like basil, chives, or dill.

PER SERVING: 125 CALORIES | 1 G CARBOHYDRATE (0 G FIBER | 0 G ADDED SUGARS | 1 G NET CARBS) | 15 G PROTEIN | 7 G FAT | 216 MG SODIUM

Chicken Turmeric Burgers

Simple pantry ingredients join forces to create a phenomenal taste with great depth. These burgers taste delicious served in lettuce wraps with a drizzle of liquid aminos, a dab of mayo, or Sriracha chili sauce.

TOTAL PREP AND COOK TIME: 20 minutes

YIELD: 4 servings, 2 patties each

1 pound (455 g) ground chicken

¼ cup (40 g) finely chopped onion

1 clove garlic, minced

1 teaspoon ground ginger

½ teaspoon ground turmeric or curry powder

¼ teaspoon salt

Freshly ground black pepper, to taste

1 tablespoon + 1 teaspoon (20 ml) extra-virgin olive oil, divided

1. In a bowl, combine the chicken, onion, garlic, ginger, turmeric or curry powder, salt, and pepper, using your hands or a wooden spoon to distribute the seasonings evenly.
2. Heat a large sauté pan, skillet, or griddle over medium heat. Add 1 tablespoon (15 ml) of the oil.
3. Using a ¼-cup (60 g) measuring cup, scoop the chicken into the pan, molding each into thin patties, about 3 inches (7.5 cm) wide. You should get 8 patties. Brown on one side, about 3 minutes. Flip and brown the other side, about 2 minutes. If you still have chicken left to cook, scrape any bits from the pan. Place the pan back on the heat and add the remaining 1 teaspoon (5 ml) oil. Cook the remaining patties.

RECIPE NOTE

Turmeric is a single-ingredient spice, contrary to curry powder, a seasoning blend that uses turmeric as a main ingredient. Keep a small bottle of turmeric on hand for mixing into chicken salad, simmering curry dishes, and stirring into turmeric lattes.

PER SERVING: 206 CALORIES | 1 G CARBOHYDRATE (0 G FIBER | 0 G ADDED SUGARS | 1 G NET CARBS) | 20 G PROTEIN | 14 G FAT | 213 MG SODIUM

Grilled Chicken Quarters with Oregano and Lemon

Bone-in, skin-on chicken quarters, made up of the thigh and leg, are a favorite classic Sunday dinner. The skin becomes browned and crackly. When grilling chicken such as this, aim to keep the heat of the grill moderate so you don't burn the skin before the chicken cooks through. You can either cook the chicken right away, or for a more intense lemony taste, marinate it for a few hours.

TOTAL PREP AND COOK TIME: 30 minutes

YIELD: 4 servings, 1 leg or 1 thigh

1 pound (455 g) chicken quarters (or thighs and drumsticks), trimmed

1 lemon, zest finely grated, plus 2 tablespoons (30 ml) juice

1 tablespoon (15 ml) extra-virgin olive oil

1 teaspoon dried oregano

1 clove garlic, smashed with wide side of knife

¼ teaspoon salt

Freshly ground black pepper, to taste

1. Cut the quarters through the joint, dividing the thigh from the leg. Place the chicken in a dish and cover with the lemon zest and juice, oil, oregano, garlic, salt, and pepper.
2. When ready to cook the chicken, preheat a grill to 375° to 400°F (190° to 200°C). Place the chicken on the grill, skin-side down, and cook until the skin is browned and the chicken is cooked nearly halfway through, about 10 minutes. Turn the chicken and cook through, about 5 minutes, or until an internal temperature thermometer reads 165°F (73°C). Remove and allow the chicken to rest for about 5 minutes before cutting.

Make It for the Whole Family

After rubbing the chicken with the oil, just sprinkle salt on a portion for kids or picky eaters.

PER SERVING: 161 CALORIES | 1 G CARBOHYDRATE (0 G FIBER | 0 G ADDED SUGARS | 1 G NET CARBS) | 18 G PROTEIN | 9 G FAT | 222 MG SODIUM

Herb-Marinated Chicken Breasts

This recipe can be made with whatever fresh herbs you happen to have on hand. It's easy, lean, and delicious. The chicken can also be quickly grilled or broiled. You can slice the leftovers and serve them over a salad made of spinach and arugula, cherry tomatoes, shredded carrots, fresh peas, and corn. This marinade also works well with turkey breasts and firm-fleshed fish.

TOTAL PREP AND COOK TIME: 25 minutes, plus 1 to 2 hours for marinating **YIELD:** 4 servings

½ cup (120 ml) fresh lemon juice

¼ cup (60 ml) extra-virgin olive oil

4 cloves garlic, minced

2 tablespoons (5 g) chopped fresh basil

1 tablespoon (4 g) chopped fresh oregano

1 tablespoon (6 g) chopped fresh mint

2 pounds (910 g) chicken breast tenders

½ teaspoon unrefined sea salt or salt

¼ teaspoon freshly ground black pepper

1. In a small bowl, whisk the lemon juice, olive oil, garlic, basil, oregano, and mint well to combine. Place the chicken breasts in a large shallow bowl or glass baking pan, and pour the dressing over the top.
2. Cover, place in the refrigerator, and allow to marinate for 1 to 2 hours. Remove from the refrigerator, and season with the salt and pepper.
3. Heat a large, wide skillet over medium-high heat. Using tongs, place the chicken tenders evenly in the bottom of the skillet. Pour the remaining marinade over the chicken.
4. Allow to cook for 3 to 5 minutes each side, or until the chicken is golden, juices have been absorbed, and meat is cooked to an internal temperature of 160°F (71°C).

Mediterranean Tradition

You'll find lemon juice used as an ingredient or as a garnish in most fish and poultry recipes in the region. In addition to the taste and moisture that the citrus juice adds to the recipe, lemon's antibacterial properties are coveted for killing bad bacteria in undercooked foods, making them both safe and delicious to eat.

PER SERVING: 410 CALORIES | 3 G CARBOHYDRATE (0 G FIBER | 0 G ADDED SUGARS | 3 G NET CARBS) | 51 G PROTEIN | 20 G FAT | 400 MG SODIUM

Baked Chicken with Nutty Dukkah Crust

Dukkah, pronounced DOO-kah, is a seasoning blend originating in Egypt. This recipe was created to yield a couple extra tablespoons of seasoning to reserve for other recipes, because once you taste this, you'll want to sprinkle it on everything from dips to snacks to fish to side dishes.

TOTAL PREP AND COOK TIME: 30 minutes **YIELD:** 5 servings

¼ cup (31 g) shelled, roasted pistachios

2 tablespoons (18 g) toasted sesame seeds

1¼ teaspoons (2 g) coriander seeds

½ teaspoon black peppercorns

1½ teaspoons ground cumin

½ teaspoon salt

1¼ pounds (568 g) chicken thighs or breasts, pounded to ½ inch (13 mm) thick, cut into 5 servings

1 tablespoon (15 ml) extra-virgin olive oil

1. Preheat the oven to 400°F (200°C, or gas mark 6) convection (if available). Line a baking sheet with parchment paper.
2. Place the pistachios, sesame seeds, coriander, and peppercorns into a small food processor or personal-size blender. Process the ingredients until the pistachios are ground into small pieces, but not to a paste, a few seconds. Stir in the ground cumin and salt. Reserve 2 tablespoons (16 g) seasoning in a sealed container for use at a later time.
3. Coat the chicken completely in the remaining ground seasoning blend. Lay the chicken on the prepared baking sheet and drizzle with the olive oil. Bake until cooked through, about 12 minutes.

SUGGESTIONS AND VARIATIONS

Traditional dukkah also contains hazelnuts. If you happen to have some on hand, feel free to use half pistachios, half hazelnuts in this recipe.

RECIPE NOTE

Alternatively, you may cook the seasoned chicken on the stovetop: Heat a sauté pan over medium heat. Add the oil and when it is hot, add the chicken and cook about halfway through on the first side, but before the seasonings burn, about 3 minutes. Turn and cook through, about 3 minutes.

PER SERVING: 204 CALORIES | 3 G CARBOHYDRATE (1 G FIBER | 0 G ADDED SUGARS | 2 G NET CARBS) | 27 G PROTEIN | 9 G FAT | 270 MG SODIUM

Make It for the Whole Family

If you think your kids will hesitate trying the chicken with the dukkah seasoning, reserve a piece of chicken and cut it into nuggets. Sprinkle with salt and drizzle with olive oil, baking it on the same baking sheet, but in a different section, about 10 minutes.

Roasted Chicken with Herbes de Provence and Lemon

Use fresh, not frozen, chicken for this when you can, which will yield juicier results. This chicken dish is great for Sunday dinners.

TOTAL PREP AND COOK TIME: 45 minutes **YIELD:** 6 servings, 1 piece each, size varies

3 pounds (1.4 kg) chicken parts, skin on (such as 2 breasts, 2 thighs, and 2 legs)

1 lemon, zest finely grated, then fruit cut in half

1 or 2 cloves garlic, thinly sliced

1 tablespoon (15 ml) extra-virgin olive oil

1 teaspoon kosher salt

2 tablespoons (11 g) dried herbes de Provence

1. Preheat the oven to 375°F (190°C, or gas mark 5). Line a baking sheet with parchment paper.
2. Pat the chicken dry. Slide the lemon zest and garlic under the skin of the chicken. Place the chicken on the prepared baking sheet, drizzle with the oil, and sprinkle with the salt and herbes de Provence. Roast for 25 to 30 minutes, until the edges are sizzling and cooked through. Allow the chicken to rest for 5 minutes before cutting. Spritz with half of the lemon.

PER SERVING: 306 CALORIES | 0 G CARBOHYDRATE (0 G FIBER | 0 G ADDED SUGARS | 0 G NET CARBS) | 33 G PROTEIN | 19 G FAT | 389 MG SODIUM

Rotisserie Chicken Stew with Kale

Rotate in a rotisserie chicken every once in a while for an easy-peasy, yummy dinner. And let's face it, as soon as you bring it home is the best time to eat it. This recipe gives you a tasty way to use up the leftover chicken the next day, since simmering in broth moistens it right back up. If this will be a one-bowl dinner with no other accompaniments, the yield will be closer to 4 servings.

TOTAL PREP AND COOK TIME: 25 minutes **YIELD:** 6 servings, 1 cup (240 g) each

1 tablespoon (15 ml) extra-virgin olive oil

1 bag (5-ounce [142 g]) chopped kale

1 medium carrot, thinly sliced

2 cloves garlic, smashed with wide side of knife

3½ cups (805 ml) chicken bone broth or herbed chicken broth

½ cooked rotisserie chicken, cut into parts

Freshly ground black pepper, to taste

1. Place a large pot over medium heat. Add the oil. When the oil is shimmering, add the kale, carrot, and garlic. Sauté until the kale is mostly wilted and tender, about 5 minutes.

2. Add the broth and cook over medium-high heat to get things moving. As soon as it comes to a simmer, add the chicken parts and flavorful chicken juices from the bottom of the container. Simmer until heated through.

RECIPE NOTE

This recipe calls for the regular-size rotisserie chicken in stores, not the super-size chickens. Please make adjustments, as needed.

PER SERVING: 111 CALORIES | 2 G CARBOHYDRATE (1 G FIBER | 0 G ADDED SUGARS | 1 G NET CARBS) | 17 G PROTEIN | 4 G FAT | 207 MG SODIUM

Mediterranean Tradition

Many women in the region don't bother roasting one thing at a time. You can make at least two chickens at a time, using leftover chicken to make chicken noodle soup or chicken salad. Other times you can roast a chicken and a whole fish, which can be dressed in the same way and need only one-third of the time to bake. You can eat the fish immediately and serve the chicken later in the day or the next—with leftovers on the third day.

Roman Tavola Calda–Style Roasted Chicken with Potatoes

Tavola calda means "hot table" in Italian. The term refers to take-out establishments that specialize in rotisserie chickens and ready-to-eat hot dishes such as pizza bianca, potato croquettes, baked pasta, and more—with special twists making them unique to the region they're in. The food served in many of the tavola caldas is so delicious and satisfying that you might even prefer it to that in fine restaurants. If so, when in Rome you can purchase roasted chicken, herb-roasted potatoes, focaccia, and risotto croquettes and take them to a park, such as Villa Borghese, to enjoy.

TOTAL PREP AND COOK TIME: 2 hours **YIELD:** 8 servings

1 whole chicken (3½ pounds, or 1.6 kg), cleaned and rinsed well

¼ cup (60 ml) extra-virgin olive oil

1 teaspoon unrefined sea salt or salt

½ teaspoon freshly ground black pepper

1 tablespoon (2 g) finely chopped fresh rosemary

1 head garlic, stem sliced off, left intact

1 lemon, cut in half

1½ pounds (680 g) Yukon Gold or other potatoes, peeled and cut into 1-inch (2.5 cm) pieces

1. Preheat the oven to 425°F (220°C). Place the chicken in a roasting pan and drizzle the olive oil over the chicken, turning to make sure that both the pan and chicken are coated. Season with the salt, pepper, and rosemary by rubbing them into the top and sides of the chicken.

2. Place the garlic and 1 lemon half inside the chicken cavity, and squeeze the remaining lemon half over the chicken. Bake, uncovered, for 45 minutes. Carefully (oil tends to splatter), remove the chicken from the oven and scatter the potatoes around the edges, turning to coat in the olive oil.

3. Return to the oven to bake for another 45 minutes, or until the chicken is done and the potatoes are tender. The chicken is done when clear juices run from the thickest part of the thigh after being pierced with a fork, or when the internal temperature of the meat reaches 165°F (74°C).

4. Cover the chicken and allow to rest 10 minutes before carving. Discard the garlic and lemon from the chicken cavity before serving.

PER SERVING: 370 CALORIES | 16 G CARBOHYDRATE (2 G FIBER | 0 G ADDED SUGARS | 15 G NET CARBS) | 23 G PROTEIN | 24 G FAT | 380 MG SODIUM

Easy Asparagus Frittata

While a frittata sounds brunchy and fancy, it is seriously so easy, you'll want to make it on the regular. It's really versatile; from breakfast to lunch to dinner, it can be savored anytime during the day. It's also a wonderful way to use up any vegetable bits you have in the fridge, whether they are leftovers or raw.

TOTAL PREP AND COOK TIME: 30 minutes

YIELD: 6 servings, 1 slice each

6 large eggs

¼ cup (60 ml) milk

¼ cup (25 g) grated Parmesan cheese

¼ + ⅛ teaspoon salt

Freshly ground black pepper, to taste

½ bunch asparagus

1 tablespoon (15 ml) extra-virgin olive oil

½ cup (80 g) diced red onion

1. Whisk the eggs, milk, Parmesan, salt, and pepper in a bowl. Break off the woody bottom third or fourth from the asparagus and discard. Slice the stalks of the asparagus into small pieces, reserving the top 1 to 2 inches (2.5 to 5 cm) of the tips.

2. Heat a medium sauté pan, about 10 inches (25 cm), over medium heat. Add the oil. When the oil is shimmering, add the onions and asparagus. Sauté until the onions are translucent. Pour in the eggs. Cover and cook over medium-low heat for about 10 minutes.

SUGGESTIONS AND VARIATIONS

You can substitute the asparagus with other vegetables, like broccoli, zucchini, and mushrooms. If the vegetables are already cooked, you can add them in toward the end of cooking the onion.

Red onion can be substituted with any type of onion, like white or yellow onion, leeks, or scallions.

Make It for the Whole Family

For your picky eaters, it's not too difficult to push all of the greenery in a couple of servings out of the frittata, before you add the egg, gently pouring it into the blank space.

PER SERVING: 127 CALORIES | 4 G CARBOHYDRATE (1 G FIBER | 0 G ADDED SUGARS | 3 G NET CARBS) | 9 G PROTEIN | 9 G FAT | 297 MG SODIUM

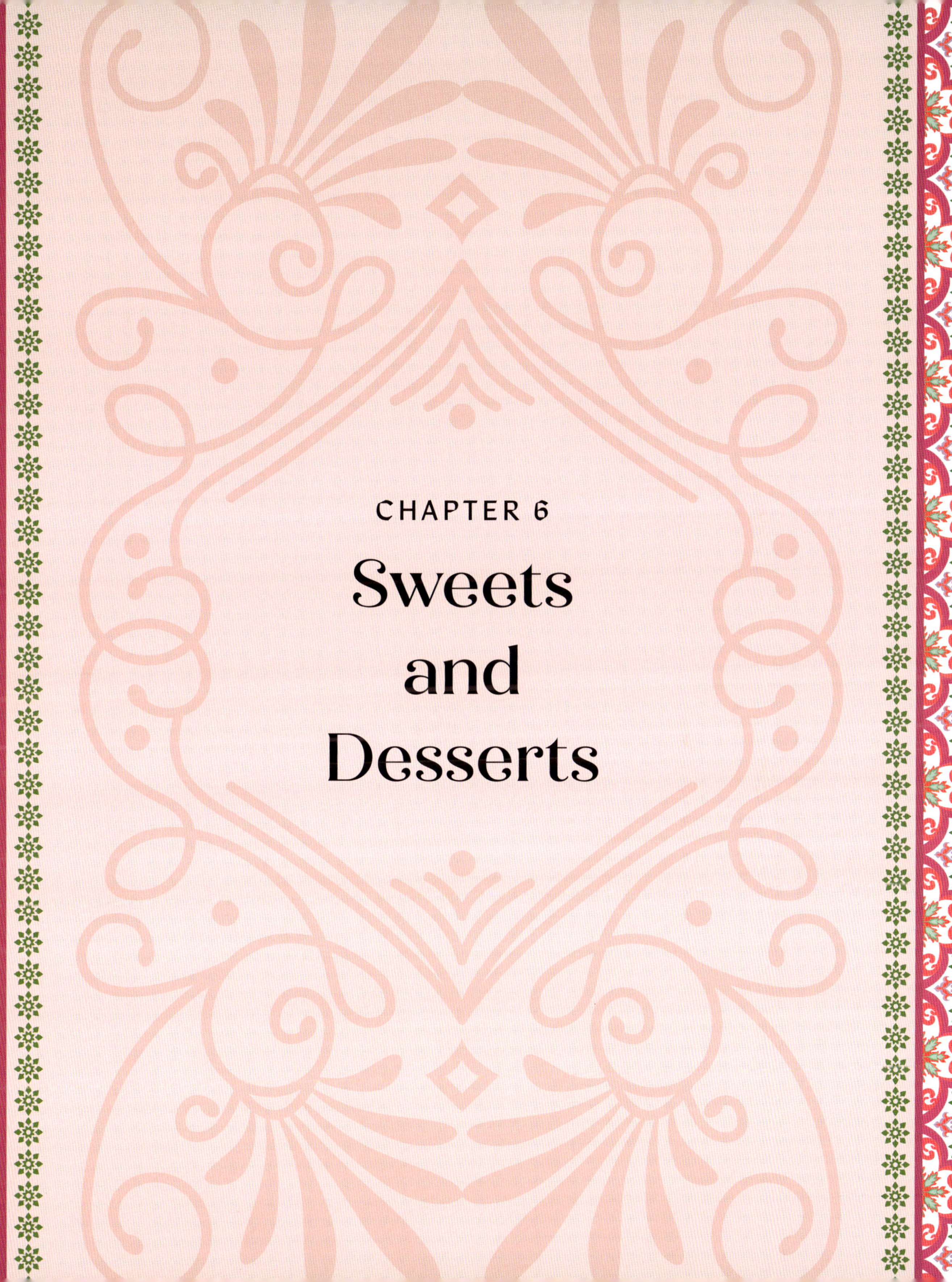

CHAPTER 6

Sweets and Desserts

Seasonal Fruit Platter

Ripe fresh fruit, enjoyed at its peak, can be so hard to come by that it is preferred over elaborate, decadent desserts. This recipe calls for a selection of summer fruits, but that doesn't mean that a fruit platter can't be served all year long. In most countries in the Mediterranean, fresh fruit completes a meal. Whether it's a plate of fresh oranges in the spring, fresh figs, dates, and grapes in the fall, or apples and pears in the winter, their flavor can't be beat. Eating seasonal fruits is healthier because they contain the nutrients our bodies need during that specific time of year.

TOTAL PREP AND COOK TIME: 20 minutes **YIELD:** 6 servings

2 cups (290 g) fresh strawberries

1 cup (145 g) chopped fresh cantaloupe

1 cup (180 g) chopped fresh honeydew melon

1 cup (165 g) chopped fresh pineapple (peeled, cored, and diced into 1-inch, or 2.5 cm, wedges)

8 kiwi, peeled and sliced into ¼-inch (6 mm) rounds

1. Arrange the fruit in a pleasing pattern on a serving plate and serve with cocktail forks or cocktail toothpicks.

Mediterranean Tradition

Local fresh fruit is easier to come by in many Mediterranean countries than it is elsewhere. For a long-term health investment, plant your own fruit trees or gardens. Even if you don't have a lot of space, some fruits, like strawberries, can be grown in containers on a terrace or balcony. By growing your own fruit, you'll save time and money while eating healthier.

PER SERVING: 110 CALORIES | 26 G CARBOHYDRATE (5 G FIBER | 0 G ADDED SUGARS | 21 G NET CARBS) | 1 G PROTEIN | 1 G FAT | 10 MG SODIUM

North African Fruit "Cocktail"

Countries from Morocco to Egypt and Turkey serve fresh fruit cocktails at street-side fruit stands. Decorated with hanging bags of ripe, fresh, seasonal fruit, they offer some of the most delicious, but fortunately not guilty, pleasures to be had. Feel free to substitute your favorite fruit trio whenever the mood strikes.

TOTAL PREP AND COOK TIME: 15 minutes | **YIELD:** 4 cocktails

1 pound (455 g) strawberries, cleaned and trimmed

¼ cup (50 g) sugar, or to taste

1 cup (235 ml) fresh orange juice

4 teaspoons (20 ml) pomegranate or other syrup

16 pomegranate arils (seeds)

1. Chill 4 clear glasses. Purée the strawberries in a blender until frothy. Add sugar, to taste, and whip until combined. Divide the strawberry juice equally among the 4 glasses.
2. Holding the back of a spoon over the strawberry juice, pour the orange juice over the top of the spoon (this prevents the 2 colors from mixing). Repeat with the other 3 glasses.
3. Pour 1 teaspoon of pomegranate syrup on top of each glass and garnish each with a few pomegranate seeds. Serve immediately.

Mediterranean Tradition

Even though these sweet fruit drinks are made in a few minutes, they are not considered a fast food. Most people stop to enjoy a fruit cocktail as part of an evening stroll with family and friends, reinforcing the popular Mediterranean trends of walking and enjoying fresh fruit after a meal, which is a healthful alternative to ice cream and TV. Look for pomegranate syrup, a condensed pomegranate juice, in Mediterranean markets.

PER SERVING: 110 CALORIES | 28 G CARBOHYDRATE (2 G FIBER | 12 G ADDED SUGARS | 25 G NET CARBS) | 1 G PROTEIN | 0 G FAT | 0 MG SODIUM

Rosé Spritz with Citrus and Mint

One sip of this light rosé spritz and you might feel like you should be on the Mediterranean. In Rovinj, Croatia (a little seaside village in the northern part of the country, in Istria—the truffle mecca), there is a wine cocktail very similar to this one. This recipe includes a few modifications to eliminate any need for simple syrups, an ingredient usually used to sweeten drinks.

TOTAL PREP AND COOK TIME: 10 minutes **YIELD:** 1 serving

1 large mint sprig, leaves removed from stems

2 orange slices

Crushed ice

5 ounces (150 ml) rosé wine

2 teaspoons elderflower liqueur (optional)

2 ounces (60 ml) grapefruit-flavored sparkling water

1. Place the mint leaves and orange slices in a glass (you can use a sturdy stemless wineglass). Smash them gently a few times with a muddler or wooden spoon, pressing out the juices.
2. Add the crushed ice and rosé. Top with the liqueur, if using, and sparkling water.

SUGGESTIONS AND VARIATIONS

This drink is also delicious made with dry white wine, such as Sauvignon Blanc, in place of rosé.

Make It for the Whole Family

For your kids, make mocktails with 100 percent fruit juice in place of the wine and liqueur.

PER SERVING: 140 CALORIES | 3 G CARBOHYDRATE (1 G FIBER | 0 G ADDED SUGARS | 2 G NET CARBS) | 0 G PROTEIN | 0 G FAT | 14 MG SODIUM

Fresh Mint Tea with Citrus

This hot drink is a digestif, rather than an aperitif, and is a soothing, comforting way to end the day after a meal. It's a great way to use up an abundance of fresh mint. Using a double-walled glass teacup seems to keep the drink hotter, longer.

TOTAL PREP AND COOK TIME: 10 minutes | **YIELD:** 1 serving

1 cup (240 ml) water

1 small handful fresh mint leaves

1 lime slice

1 orange slice

1. Bring the water to a boil in a kettle. Place the mint in a teacup. Pour the boiling water over the mint. Add the lime and orange slices. Cover with a saucer and allow it to steep. After a few minutes, you can start drinking it while it's hottest. Press gently on the orange and lime to release some of the juices.

2. You can remove the mint and citrus before sipping or leave them in the teacup to steep longer to develop a deeper flavor. You can push the orange slice down on the mint to keep the mint from floating up.

SUGGESTIONS AND VARIATIONS

During the winter months, you may also like to add a small cinnamon stick to the cup.

PER SERVING: 12 CALORIES | 3 G CARBOHYDRATE (1 G FIBER | 0 G ADDED SUGARS | 2 G NET CARBS) | 0 G PROTEIN | 0 G FAT | 0 MG SODIUM

Strawberry "Beauty" Smoothie

If you're looking for a beauty boost, this sweet and satisfying smoothie is just for you! Strawberries are a great way to get more fiber, vitamin C, and healthy cancer-preventing compounds into your diet. Bananas are rich in vitamins A, B, and E, making them powerful antiaging agents that are often applied directly on the skin as masks. The presence of live cultures along with lactic acid, zinc, and other minerals and enzymes in yogurt makes it a great choice for improving skin conditions as well. Flaxseed was cultivated in Babylon as early as 3000 BCE and contains a high amount of omega-3 fatty acids, which can help lower cholesterol and improve the complexion.

TOTAL PREP AND COOK TIME: 10 minutes **YIELD:** 2 servings

1 very ripe banana, sliced

1 cup (100 g) ice

1 cup (230 g) yogurt

2 tablespoons (40 g) organic honey, or to taste

1 cup (145 g) strawberries

2 tablespoons (24 g) flaxseeds

1. Blend the banana, ice, yogurt, and honey together until the banana is well blended.
2. Add the strawberries and flaxseeds and blend on low speed for 30 seconds, or until frothy. Pour into clear glasses and serve cold.

Mediterranean Tradition

Traditionally, many facial and skin-care regimens in the Mediterranean region utilized fruits as their primary ingredients. Try combining yogurt with honey and applying it over dry skin. Leave on for 20 minutes, rinse, and dry. Your skin will be extremely soft and supple.

PER SERVING: 270 CALORIES | 48 G CARBOHYDRATE (6 G FIBER | 17 G ADDED SUGARS | 42 G NET CARBS) | 9 G PROTEIN | 7 G FAT | 90 MG SODIUM

Poached Vanilla-Scented Pears and Figs

This dessert is so elegant and delicious that no one will even realize that it's good for them! Pears are a great source of dietary fiber, which lowers cholesterol and prevents colon cancer. Ounce per ounce, figs, one of the world's oldest fruits, contain more nutrients than any other fruit.

TOTAL PREP AND COOK TIME: 35 minutes **YIELD:** 4 servings

4 Bosc pears, peeled

16 dried figs

2 tablespoons (30 ml) lemon juice

2 tablespoons (40 g) honey

1 teaspoon pure vanilla bean paste or pure vanilla extract

1. Slice off the bottoms of the pears so they can stand firmly. Place the pears and figs in a medium saucepan and cover with water.
2. Add the lemon juice, honey, and vanilla paste. Bring to a boil over high heat, reduce heat to medium-low, and simmer 20 minutes, or until the pears are tender.
3. When the pears are cool enough to handle, remove them from the poaching liquid and stand them upright in the middle of 4 dessert plates.
4. Drizzle a few tablespoons of cooking liquid over the tops of the pears and arrange 4 figs around the sides of each plate.
5. Allow to stand for 5 minutes at room temperature and serve.

Mediterranean Tradition

Getting family and friends involved in preparing meals is a Mediterranean tradition worth copying. In addition to making the work easier and more pleasurable, the communal aspect of sharing a task is emotionally satisfying. You'll be less likely to order unhealthy take-out if you know that others are looking forward to cooking.

PER SERVING: 210 CALORIES | 52 G CARBOHYDRATE (9 G FIBER | 1 G ADDED SUGARS | 43 G NET CARBS) | 2 G PROTEIN | 0 G FAT | 5 MG SODIUM

Roasted Plums with Basil-Yogurt Cream

Roasting fruits enhances their sweetness and gives them a unique texture. Serving them with yogurt and herbs increases health benefits. Keep this in mind when planning desserts for yourself, friends, and family. Even though recipes such as these are simple and healthful, many people prefer their flavor to store-bought cakes and pastries.

TOTAL PREP AND COOK TIME: 45 minutes **YIELD:** 4 servings

1 teaspoon olive oil

4 ripe plums, halved and pitted

4 teaspoons (16 g) sugar

1 cup (230 g) vanilla yogurt

2 tablespoons (5 g) finely chopped fresh basil

1 teaspoon honey

1. Preheat the oven to 400°F (200°C). Oil a large baking dish. Place the plums inside, cut side up, and sprinkle ½ teaspoon sugar over each. Bake, uncovered, for 35 minutes.
2. While the plums are baking, stir together the yogurt, basil, and honey.
3. Divide half of the yogurt mixture onto each of 4 plates, or a large serving platter.
4. When the plums are finished baking, remove them from the oven and place 2 halves over the yogurt on each plate. Fill the holes with the remaining yogurt mixture and serve warm.

Mediterranean Tradition

If you're prone to skipping breakfast, prepare larger quantities of dishes such as this one in the evening. The fiber-rich plums and the protein-packed yogurt will keep you pleasantly full for hours.

PER SERVING: 120 CALORIES | 21 G CARBOHYDRATE (1 G FIBER | 9 G ADDED SUGARS | 20 G NET CARBS) | 2 G PROTEIN | 3 G FAT | 25 MG SODIUM

Apricot and Orange Blossom Pudding with Pistachios

Dairy-free fruit puddings such as this one make sweet, light, and satisfying finales to any meal. Orange blossom water can be found in Mediterranean and Middle Eastern markets, or in the baking aisle of gourmet grocery stores.

TOTAL PREP AND COOK TIME: 2 hours, 15 minutes **YIELD:** 8 servings

1 pound (455 g) dried apricots

1 cup (200 g) sugar

4 tablespoons (32 g) cornstarch dissolved in ¼ cup (60 ml) cold water

1 tablespoon (15 ml) orange blossom water

Handful of pistachios, shelled and finely chopped

1. Chop the apricots into small pieces. Place them in a large bowl and cover them with 4 cups (950 ml) of boiling water. Cover the bowl with a plate or lid. When the apricot pieces break down and nearly dissolve, add the sugar, and stir. Purée the mixture in a blender.

2. Pour the apricot juice into a medium saucepan. Add the cornstarch mixture and stir well with a wooden spoon to combine. Set the heat to high and allow the mixture to boil for 2 minutes, stirring constantly. Reduce the heat to medium-low, add the orange blossom water, and continue cooking the pudding, stirring slowly until it thickens and pulls away from the sides of the saucepan.

3. Pour into individual ramekins or a large decorative bowl. Sprinkle pistachios on top in a pattern and refrigerate about 2 hours, or until set. Serve cold.

Mediterranean Tradition

If you ever drive through the Mediterranean countryside in March or April, a thick musky, citrus aroma might start to overwhelm your senses. After a mile or two, you will pass an orange orchard. In many areas of the Mediterranean, that very scent gets preserved for year-round use in a lovely ingredient called orange blossom water. The distilled essential oils from the orange blossoms themselves get transformed into a heady, intoxicating liquid that enhances everything with just a single drop. It is used in everything from Middle Eastern baklavas to French clafoutis and Neapolitan Pastiera cakes, and some people even iron their linens with it.

PER SERVING: 280 CALORIES | 69 G CARBOHYDRATE (4 G FIBER | 25 G ADDED SUGARS | 65 G NET CARBS) | 2 G PROTEIN | 2 G FAT | 0 MG SODIUM

Grilled Peaches with Yogurt and Honey

Peaches originated in Central Asia and made their way to the Mediterranean via Silk Route trading. Any type of peach can be used to make this recipe provided that they are ripe, but not too soft. The grill's sizzling heat instantly sears the surface of the fruit upon contact, which caramelizes its sugars and enhances its natural sweetness. Frozen Greek yogurt, full of inulin, which helps balance blood sugar levels, and healing honey, complement the peach flavors perfectly.

TOTAL PREP AND COOK TIME: 20 minutes

YIELD: 4 servings

4 medium ripe peaches, cut in half (pits removed)

1 cup (245 g) plain frozen Greek yogurt

8 tablespoons (160 g) honey

Cinnamon

1. Place the peaches cut-side down on the grill. Grill on low or indirect heat until soft, 2 to 4 minutes on each side.
2. Set the peaches on a serving platter and top each with 2 tablespoons (31 g) of frozen Greek yogurt.
3. Drizzle a tablespoon (20 g) of honey over the top of each and garnish with a dash of cinnamon. Serve immediately.

Mediterranean Tradition

Always make more grilled fruit than you need for your recipe. It tastes great cut up and tossed into salads and pilafs, and it is a quick, easy way to pack extra nutrients into a meal.

PER SERVING: 220 CALORIES | 51 G CARBOHYDRATE (2 G FIBER | 34 G ADDED SUGARS | 49 G NET CARBS) | 7 G PROTEIN | 1.5 G FAT | 20 MG SODIUM

Italian Baked Apples with Cream and Amaretti

There are more than 7,000 varieties of apples in the United States alone, yet most of those available to consumers fall within one of 50 varieties. The apple was cultivated in ancient Egypt. There are many mythological associations over various civilizations, with the apple in the Garden of Eden being the most widely known. Throughout the Middle Ages in the eastern Mediterranean, people gave an apple with a bite out of it to their romantic interests. This classic Italian recipe is easy enough to be enjoyed anytime, but elegant enough for entertaining.

TOTAL PREP AND COOK TIME: 45 minutes **YIELD:** 6 servings

1 tablespoon (14 g) butter

6 apples, cored

1 cup (236 ml) heavy cream, divided

¼ cup (50 g) sugar

6 ounces (170 ml) amaretti, or other gluten-free cookies

1. Preheat the oven to 350°F (180°C) and grease a 9-inch (23 cm) baking pan with butter.
2. Place the apples in the baking pan and add water to a depth of ⅛ inch (3 mm). Place in the oven and bake, uncovered, until the apples are tender but still firm, about 30 minutes. Remove from the oven and let cool.
3. Heat ½ cup (118 ml) of the cream and the sugar in a medium saucepan over medium heat until boiling, stirring with a wooden spoon. When the sugar has dissolved, set aside to cool for 5 minutes.
4. Whip the remaining ½ cup (118 ml) cream until firm. Reserve half of the whipped cream for decorating. With a spatula, fold the remaining ¼ cup whipped cream into the cooled cream and sugar mixture.
5. Arrange the apples in a deep serving dish. Pour the cream sauce over them and pipe the reserved whipped cream around them. Crumble the amaretti cookies and sprinkle over the tops of the apples.

PER SERVING: 380 CALORIES | 53 G CARBOHYDRATE (5 G FIBER | 25 G ADDED SUGARS | 49 G NET CARBS) | 2 G PROTEIN | 18 G FAT | 53 MG SODIUM

Mediterranean Tradition

The high fiber content in apples makes them a rich source of soluble fiber, which helps prevent the build-up of cholesterol in blood vessels and reduces the risk of heart attack. Apple peels are especially good choices for diabetics because they help to slow down the rate that sugar is absorbed in the blood. In addition to being eaten raw, apples are a great alternative to potatoes in stews, taste great in salads, and make fantastic desserts.

Crispy Oven-Dried Orange Slices

These wispy things have a concentrated, intense orange flavor that will leave you obsessed. You can try them as a drink garnish, but make sure you don't let it fall into the drink! Enjoy them as is for a sweet treat, or serve with cheese.

TOTAL PREP AND COOK TIME: 45 minutes **YIELD:** 8 servings

2 oranges

4 teaspoons (28 g) honey

⅛ teaspoon ground cinnamon

2 teaspoons warm water

1. Preheat the oven to 300°F (150°C, or gas mark 2). Line 2 baking sheets with parchment paper or a silicone baking mat.
2. Using a serrated knife, cut the oranges crosswise into ⅛-inch (3 mm) slices. You should get 8 slices per orange. Remove the seeds. Spread out the oranges on the prepared baking sheets.
3. Combine the honey, cinnamon, and water in a small bowl, and brush this mixture generously onto the oranges. Shake the pan gently back and forth to distribute the honey underneath the oranges. Bake until bubbling around the edges and appearing slightly dried out, about 30 minutes. Let cool. Store in an airtight container.

PER SERVING: 100 CALORIES | 13 G CARBOHYDRATE (2 G FIBER | 0 G ADDED SUGARS | 11 G NET CARBS) | 7 G PROTEIN | 3 G FAT | 500 MG SODIUM

Crunchy Almond Clusters

These small but satisfying petits fours are a great way to enjoy daily morning espresso drinks while staying in Rovinj, Croatia, at Hotel Lone. You can look forward to them every morning.

TOTAL PREP AND COOK TIME: 30 minutes **YIELD:** 32 servings, 1 each

2 egg whites

½ cup (100 g) sugar

½ teaspoon almond extract

3 cups (330 g) sliced almonds

1. Preheat the oven to 350°F (180°C, or gas mark 4). Line a baking sheet with parchment paper.
2. In a clean bowl, beat the egg whites and sugar with a mixer on high speed until soft peaks form. Add the almond extract and mix again quickly. Fold in the almonds.
3. Using a tablespoon (15 g) scoop, spoon the mixture onto the prepared baking sheet. You should get 32 cookies. Bake in batches until golden, about 12 minutes. Cool completely before storing in a sealed container.

PER SERVING: 64 CALORIES | 8 G CARBOHYDRATE (1 G FIBER | 3 G ADDED SUGARS | 4 G NET CARBS) | 2 G PROTEIN | 4 G FAT | 4 MG SODIUM

Grilled Watermelon with Goat Cheese and Mint

Watermelon is the ultimate thirst quencher and palate cleanser during the dead of summer. People are surprised to hear that 1 cup (150 g) of watermelon is only 11 grams carbs. Watermelon is largely composed of—you guessed it—water.

TOTAL PREP AND COOK TIME: 30 minutes **YIELD:** 4 servings

¼ cup (60 ml) balsamic vinegar

1 teaspoon honey

4 thick watermelon wedges, rind on

1 tablespoon (15 ml) extra-virgin olive oil

⅛ teaspoon salt

4 ounces (115 g) soft goat cheese

¼ cup (8 g) mint leaves, coarsely chopped

1. Preheat the grill to medium-high heat, about 400°F (200°C).
2. Pour the balsamic into a small saucepan and bring to a simmer over medium heat. Simmer until the balsamic reduces by approximately half, about 4 minutes. Remove from the heat and stir in the honey.
3. Brush the watermelon with the oil and sprinkle with the salt. Place the watermelon on the hot grill and cook until you see grill marks, about 5 minutes. Turn, and make grill marks on the other side, about 3 minutes. Remove and cut off the rind.
4. Place one piece of watermelon on a plate. Spread with some of the goat cheese, place another slice of watermelon on top, and spread with more goat cheese. Drizzle with the balsamic and sprinkle with the mint.

PER SERVING: 158 CALORIES | 13 G CARBOHYDRATE (1 G FIBER | 1 G ADDED SUGARS | 11 G NET CARBS) | 6 G PROTEIN | 10 G FAT | 207 MG SODIUM

Burrata Cheese with Balsamic-Marinated Strawberries

If you're a cheese lover, you will fully appreciate the extra creaminess of this Italian cheese, consisting of a mozzarella shell encasing oozy, thick cream. It has so many applications: as an appetizer, plopped on a salad, melted over pasta, and yes, as a final course. Because why not? But try to cut into only the amount of burrata you will use in one sitting, as you will lose the tender consistency over time once the package is open and the cheese is cut.

In this recipe, you can dress up the burrata with marinated strawberries. Make sure you're only using fragrant and sweet strawberries, trimming off any white shoulders.

TOTAL PREP AND COOK TIME: 30 minutes **YIELD:** 4 servings

1 cup (170 g) diced strawberries

1 tablespoon (15 ml) balsamic vinegar

2 teaspoons honey

¼ cup (36 g) sliced almonds, optional

Fresh basil leaves

1 large (8-ounce [226 g]) ball burrata or 2 small (4-ounce [113 g]) balls

1. In a bowl, combine the strawberries, balsamic, and honey.
2. If you are adding almonds, toast them in a dry sauté pan over medium-low heat, stirring frequently, a few minutes, reducing the heat to low as needed.
3. For the basil leaves, there are two different ways you can prepare them. Either snip the tiny leaves and use them whole. Or stack larger leaves, roll them the wide way, and thinly slice into ribbons using a sharp knife or kitchen shears.
4. When ready to serve, drain the burrata. If serving buffet-style, leave the burrata whole and place it in the center of a platter. If plating individually, cut into portions. Spoon on the strawberries and juices. Sprinkle with the almonds and basil.

SUGGESTIONS AND VARIATIONS

For a more savory preparation, use ripe, quartered tomatoes instead of strawberries. Omit the honey and sprinkle with sea salt.

PER SERVING: 221 CALORIES | 11 G CARBOHYDRATE (2 G FIBER | 3 G ADDED SUGARS | 6 G NET CARBS) | 8 G PROTEIN | 18 G FAT | 77 MG SODIUM

Prosciutto and Peaches

The antipasto of prosciutto and cantaloupe is a familiar one to Americans who frequent Italian restaurants, but wrapping peaches in prosciutto, *prosciutto e pesca*, is how this recipe does it. The success of this preparation rests on your obtaining prosciutto di Parma, the best cured ham, and the sweetest, ripest peaches, and, probably most importantly, that you wrap the peaches just before serving them. If you peel the peaches by plunging them in boiling water, it will affect their taste, so try to plunge them in for just seconds and not minutes.

TOTAL PREP AND COOK TIME: 30 minutes | **YIELD:** 30 wrapped pieces, about 10 servings

3 pounds ripe peaches, peeled if desired and pitted

½ pound thinly sliced prosciutto di Parma

1. Cut the peaches into wedges and wrap each one in a slice of prosciutto. Serve at room temperature.

PER SERVING: 100 CALORIES | 13 G CARBOHYDRATE (2 G FIBER | 0 G ADDED SUGARS | 11 G NET CARBS) | 7 G PROTEIN | 3 G FAT | 500 MG SODIUM

Photo Credits

Shutterstock on pages 2, 5, 6, 9, 10, 13, 19, 29, 30, 33, 34, 37, 41, 42, 50, 58, 62, 65, 66, 68, 70, 73, 81, 82, 86, 89, 90, 93, 97, 98, 102, 105, 107, 110, 113, 123, 131, 135, 139, 140, 143, 144, 148, 151, 152, 155, 158, 160, 163, 165, 166, 170, 173, 174, 177, 178, 181, 182

Glenn Scott Photography and styling Natasha Taylor on pages 20, 23, 25, 39, 61, 101, 116, 120, 24, 127, 128, 169

Photography and styling Richard Swearinger on pages 45, 46, 49, 53, 54, 74, 132, 186

Photography and styling Jo Harding (modernfoodstories.com) on pages 77, 78, 94, 108, 119, 136, 147, 185

Index

T

V

W

Y

Z